PETER SHAFFER

The Gift of the Gorgon

VIKING

VIKING

Published by the Penguin Group
Penguin Books Ltd, 27 Wrights Lane, London w8 5tz, England
Penguin Books USA Inc., 375 Hudson Street, New York, New York 10014, USA
Penguin Books Australia Ltd, Ringwood, Victoria, Australia
Penguin Books Canada Ltd, 10 Alcorn Avenue, Toronto, Ontario, Canada m4v 3b2
Penguin Books (NZ) Ltd, 182–190 Wairau Road, Auckland 10, New Zealand

Penguin Books Ltd, Registered Offices: Harmondsworth, Middlesex, England

First published 1993
3 5 7 9 10 8 6 4

Copyright © Venticelli Inc., 1993

The moral right of the author has been asserted

All inquiries regarding professional rights (with the exception of repertory
rights) should be addressed to Macnaughton Lowe Representation Ltd of
200 Fulham Road, London sw10 9pn

Amateur and professional repertory rights in this play are handled by
Samuel French Ltd of 52 Fitzroy Street, London w1p 6jr

Filmset in 11.25/13.5 pt Monophoto Bembo
Typeset by Datix International Limited, Bungay, Suffolk
Printed in England by Clays Ltd, St Ives plc

A CIP catalogue record for this book is available from the British Library

isbn 0–670–85069–1

To
ROBERT LANTZ
and
ELIZABETH IRELAND MCCANN
with great love
. . .
And to
the dearest memory
of
ROBERT LEONARD

INTRODUCTION

For a director, the collaboration with a playwright on a new play is the most exciting – and dangerous – activity that the theatre can offer. A director always has his own editorial function in the last stages of a production: he refines the performances, calculates the rhythm and tempo of the scene, even assesses the atmospheric quality of the lighting and the sound. He does so on the premise that everything must communicate if it is to take up the audience's time. The effect may be nice, but it must always be tested by asking if it is strictly necessary. With a new play this editorial function extends to the text itself, and this is where the danger comes in. Nobody likes criticism, particularly of something that has been carefully considered and lovingly polished. The play-wright needs to be as open and as confident as an actor if he is to accept direction. There is in my experience no one more ready to listen and to use every perception that the director can offer than Peter Shaffer.

The old Broadway rule that playwrights should be neither seen nor heard and should definitely be kept out of rehearsals is not something that I have ever endorsed. It seems to me a decision born of defensiveness. The director and the cast are the servants of the playwright: he must therefore be the centre of the collaboration. He should always be at rehearsal if he can be.

For forty years, I have observed a very simple rule: as the director I can say anything I like about the text, but it remains the playwright's prerogative to make the final decision. In exchange, the playwright can make any comment about the production but the final decision rests with me. Given trust, this pact works beautifully with every kind of dramatist, whether he is Samuel Beckett, Edward Albee, Harold Pinter, Tennessee Williams or John Guare. Or Peter Shaffer.

There are no rules for playwrights or for playwriting. Harold Pinter, for instance, delivers a script which is polished down to the last comma. I have had in my time a phone call from Pinter announcing a rewrite. It turned out to be the deletion of a pause. This is not as absurd as it sounds. Pinter's pauses represent specific crisis points in the lives of his characters; they are often moments when the characters experience major transformations. They are as crucial as major speeches.

Harold Pinter rewrites very little in rehearsal. By contrast, Peter Shaffer rewrites constantly – not because he is uncertain or mistaken in his first version, but because he is using all his skills to make the play's meaning clearer and sharper. And in this process, he needs the collaboration of his director. He calls it – somewhat diffidently – carving the play with actors. To change the metaphor, his first rehearsal scripts are huge, bold and vivid – always too long and frequently excessive. The detail and the subtle gradations of colour are found as the work proceeds. But the first version in its energy informs all the work.

We worked fiercely on *Amadeus* for its rehearsal period in London and subsequently continued to talk creatively during its run of over a year at the National Theatre. The process went on even more feverishly during the rehearsal and try-out in America: as a result the play became more focused and its impact sharper, the climactic scene changing altogether. Indeed, during the final weeks in Washington prior to its transfer to New York, Peter actually rewrote and I staged five different such scenes in as many days: as productive a collaboration as could exist between writer and director.

One method of playwriting is not superior to another. But

for a director, a rehearsal period with Peter Shaffer is an unforgettable experience because he is not just the playwright's interpreter, he is frequently the nurse in attendance at the creative act itself.

Peter told me about *The Gift of the Gorgon* some five years ago. With its bold juxtapositions of the mythic and the modern, it seemed a huge undertaking, and a wonderfully ambitious task for a man already in his sixties – a time when most dramatists are not seeking new quests but are content to sit and collect their royalties. Peter worked on it himself over a period of three years before we met and read it to each other. At the Royal Shakespeare Company in October 1992 we continued carving the play with the inspired assistance of Judi Dench, Michael Pennington and Jeremy Northam. The work was hard and challenging but virtually every day brought a reward.

We opened in December and had the most stimulating of receptions: genuine controversy. As one major critic praised the play highly for extending the boundaries of theatre, another hailed it as a turkey for Christmas. Shaffer has always divided the critics. His blend of genuine popular drama with subjects that question the conventional morality of the age has constantly aroused extravagant fury as well as extravagant praise.

In *The Gift of the Gorgon*, Shaffer once more poses a key question: what do we *feel* about terrorists? How can we deal with them – and with our feelings of rage and revenge? And, as an extension, is the theatre still a place where such issues can be debated as they were by the Greeks?

I believe this play contains some of Shaffer's best writing, particularly when he is dealing with the age-old potency of the theatre. He has also perfected for it a technique which began with *Equus* and was refined in *Amadeus*. In *The Gift of the Gorgon*, his scenes between three characters often exist in two places and in three separate times. This is a brilliant structural development which needs the utmost virtuosity by the actors playing the scene. It is much like playing a fully edited, finished film. The characters change place, time and emotion in a split second. Possibly an audience unused to the jump-cuts and sudden transitions of the modern screen would not easily understand this new technique. But Shaffer has used the cinematic sophistication of his audience to reinforce an old strength of the theatre: its ability to invite an audience to imagine. Paradoxically this is something the cinema can never do: the images remain what they are – literal. It is for the theatre to be a place of metaphors.

This play amply repays study and performance. It is innovative in technique and provocative in subject matter. It is both funny and 'terrible', as the Greeks would have it. If I say that I believe this text is the first version, it is because I know that the work will continue on one of the most original and ambitious plays of the last decade.

I have been privileged to be part of it and I must thank Peter Shaffer for another intensely alive period of work, and for asking me once again to be his director.

Peter Hall
February 1993

ACKNOWLEDGEMENTS

As I write, this play is about to transfer from the confines of The Pit Theatre in the Barbican Centre to the far more commodious space of Wyndham's. Inevitably the move will involve re-designing and re-staging, and may also involve rewriting. One of the many benefits of composing live drama is that one can alter details of the work after its initial appearance, either when a change of cast intervenes or, as in this case, a change of theatre. Of course one hopes to keep alterations to the minimum but it is not possible to perceive in advance what improvements may be suggested by the process of re-rehearsal in light of three months' playing of the script and of a new and totally different space. Publishers of plays are always indulgent over this, and I can only hope that readers will be the same. *The Gift of the Gorgon* took a very long time to write – it occupied me for three creatively intense years – and I suspect that in some important areas it may still be evolving in my head.

As regards the stage directions, I have to say that in my work, text and treatment tend to be indissoluble, and I like as far as is possible to record the main features of a first production. The play was brought to the stage with the most vigilant confidence by Peter Hall, applying a technique of rare bravura to a work which he cherished with passionate approval. It is only right that I commemorate here this act of directorial dedication, which emerged from eight weeks' rehearsal and innumerable conversations between us, to such startling effect.

My huge thanks are also due to John Gunter, a superb

ACKNOWLEDGEMENTS

designer; to Judith Weir who composed the score for the play with such expert flair; and deeply to Judi Dench and Michael Pennington, and to Jeremy Northam, for their unflagging encouragement and kindness and skill. I bless the English theatre which can still produce such talent.

Peter Shaffer
February 1993

The Gift of the Gorgon was first produced on 5 December 1992 by the Royal Shakespeare Company at The Pit Theatre in the Barbican Centre, with the following cast:

Edward Damson *a playwright*	Michael Pennington
Helen Damson *his wife*	Judi Dench
Philip *his son*	Jeremy Northam
Damsinski *his father*	Michael Poole
Jarvis *Helen's father*	Edward Jewesbury
Katina *Helen's housekeeper*	Helen Blatch
Mary	Lucy Bayler
Else	Ella Kenion
Jo-Beth	Lesley McGuire

Other parts played by Paul McLain, Simon Packham and members of the company
Radio announcements by Brian Perkins

Directed by	Peter Hall
Designed by	John Gunter
Lighting designed by	Rick Fisher
Music by	Judith Weir
Choreography by	Terry John Bates
Assistant director	Gillian Diamond
Sound designed by	Paul Arditti
Dialect coach	Jill McCullough
Company voice work by	Barbara Houseman and Andrew Wade

ACKNOWLEDGEMENTS

The musical score featured the voices of Frances Lynch and Andrew Gallacher, members of the Vocem Electric Voice Theatre

Stage Manager	Jane Pole
Deputy Stage Manager	Martin Christopher
Assistant Stage Manager	Flip Tanner

The action takes place in Edward Damson's villa on the Greek island of Thera and, in recall, England during the years 1975 to 1993.

THE SET

A space which basically represents the living-room of a Greek island villa and — divided from it upstage by transparent sliding screens — a terrace, presumed to overlook the Aegean Sea. Beyond this hangs a huge wall of grey lava, which can part centrally into halves, as can the screens. The floor of the stage is a brilliant white. The only remarkable piece of furniture visible is an impressive nineteenth-century Russian desk having a flat, green marble top and legs decorated with ormolu: Edward's desk — a place of work and inspiration, also in his mind a stage — for which purpose it is actually used by his characters. From its drawers — especially those upstage — props can be extracted: the playwright's special paper, his manuscripts, glasses, bottles of vodka and wine, and his mat-knife.

This space will also be used to represent other spaces in recall — Cambridge and Kilburn, Chelsea, Mycenae — as well as settings for Edward's plays. It must therefore be somewhat abstract, without of course destroying the illusion of naturalistic reality in the Damson villa. Half a dozen neutral chairs are consequently its other main feature. There are also, upstage, a coat rack in the extreme corner and, downstage, a large wicker basket containing academic books and periodicals which have been dumped into it.

NOTE

The Perseus episodes and the extracts from Edward's plays are all mimed by masked actors, sometimes to taped voices. Perseus is always spoken by Edward, Athena by Helen.

A PRACTICAL NOTE ON DOUBLING

The actress playing Katina can also mime the Empress Irene. The actor playing Damsinski can also mime (and speak on tape) Cromwell. The three girl tourists can also mime the Goddess Athena and her two attendant spirits, and (unmasked, of course) the hired cook, maid and secretary. One of them can dance as the exulting kidnapper in *I.R.E.*

In addition, two male actors can take the parts of Byzantine and Cromwellian soldiers: one can also play Perseus, the other the Irish terrorist. Both of them, together with the two fathers, can bear off the coffin at the start of the play.

CHARACTERS

Edward Damson   A playwright
Helen Damson   His wife
Philip   His son
Damsinski   His father
Jarvis   Helen's father
Katina   Helen's housekeeper
Else
Mary }   Girl tourists
Jo-Beth

In the Perseus scenes
    Perseus
    Athena
    Two attendant spirits

In the scenes from *Icons*
    The Empress Irene
    Constantine VI, her son
    Two guards

In the scenes from *Prerogative*
    Oliver Cromwell
    Two soldiers

In the scene from *I.R.E.*
    A terrorist
    An unnamed woman, his captor

ACT ONE

SCENE ONE

Before the play begins we see a large closed coffin, resting on top of the desk.

> [*Darkness. A wind blowing. Light comes up on the coffin. Beside it stand* HELEN, *veiled in black,* KATINA *and four Greek villagers all in silhouette. The voice of a B.B.C. commentator is heard.*]

COMMENTATOR: The death was announced last night of the playwright Edward Damson. He was forty-six. He appears to have died from an accidental fall near his villa on the Greek island of Thera. His body was found naked, badly cut from its roll down a steep cliff of lava for which the island is famous.

Damson first achieved prominence in the late seventies with his play *Icons* set in Byzantium and employing an enormous cast. *Icons* was followed by *Prerogative*, an even more elaborate piece about Oliver Cromwell, filled with scenes of extreme action.

Damson was an extreme personality, who made many extreme statements. 'It is the *duty* of the playwright,' he once declared, 'to *be* extreme. To astound his audience – and, if necessary, appal it.'

> [*The villagers lift the coffin and walk off solemnly with it.*]

His last play was obsessed with terrorism, especially in Northern Ireland. Called *I.R.E.*, it caused a scandal. Immediately afterwards the playwright retired to the Greek island he never left again in five years, seeing no visitors and answering no letters.

I

He leaves behind him a widow.

[HELEN, *standing by the desk, unveils.* KATINA, HELEN's *housekeeper – a scowling, older Greek woman wearing traditional black – enters and hands* HELEN *a letter. She opens the envelope and reads. Light up downstage on* PHILIP *speaking as she does so. He is a nervous academic of twenty-eight. English but dressed in American professional clothes: button-down shirt, bow-tie and moccasins.*]

PHILIP [*nervously*]: Dear Stepmother – Helen being regrettably still too familiar – A month has gone by since you wrote that kind letter. As I said in my reply, I would never have written to you, even in condolence, if I hadn't first received that assurance you knew I existed. Let me now be crass. I have a request, which I offer very much in fear and trembling. I would dearly like to fly from America to visit you. What I need is your consent for me to write a book. His life. I realize this may seem appallingly self-promoting. All I ask is a chance to be allowed to explain myself in person.

[*She crumples the letter.* PHILIP *sits, producing her reply.*]

HELEN [*firmly, as he reads it*]: Dear Philip, I am not seeing people now. I trust you understand. Helen Damson.

[KATINA *picks up an armful of new books which she tumbles unceremoniously into the basket.* HELEN *produces another letter and reads it silently.*]

PHILIP: Please forgive me for writing again. I'm sure I'm just as importunate as all the other Professors of Drama. I imagine they're besieging you in droves, pelting you with their books as proof of ability . . . Well, I've only got one to my name – the dissertation I sent over last year – and I'm only an *assistant* professor. But I *know* my need to write this has got to be greater than any of theirs.

[*Again she crumples the letter.*]

HELEN: I'm sorry, but I have to say no. I'm not receiving anyone at this time.

PHILIP [*insistently*]: Could I come then in the spring break? I've worked it all out. There are cheap flights from here – and then there's just the boat trip from Athens. According to my travel guide I'd have to take a donkey up the cliff face when I arrive, but there is literally nothing I wouldn't dare, to present my case! . . . Please, Stepmother, won't you relent?

[HELEN *stands rigid.*]

HELEN [*sharply*]: For the last time, I cannot see you! Understand this, please. No more letters.

[*She moves away out on to the terrace. A pause. Then impulsively* PHILIP *rises, snatches his suitcase and a briefcase, and marches determinedly across the stage. We hear the sound of a jet plane, loud. Light changes to evening in the Aegean.* KATINA *stands, barring his way. She speaks only Greek.*]

KATINA: *Ohi! Ti thelis etho?* (No! What do you want here?)

PHILIP [*nervously consulting the dictionary*]: *Kalispera* . . . I think that's right. Good-evening?

[*He smiles nervously.* KATINA *glares.*]

I am Philip Damson. I would like to see Mrs Damson.

KATINA: *Then ghinette.* (It is not possible.)

PHILIP: I have come a long way. The middle of America! I wrote to her . . . I am the son of Edward Damson.

KATINA: Eh?

PHILIP: Kyrios Damson was my father! . . . *Pateras!*

KATINA: *Then katalaveno. Prepi na fighis!* (I don't understand. You must go away!)

PHILIP [*producing a letter*]: Listen, just take this to her. *Please!* [*He finds some money.*] I wait here.

[*She stares at him with suspicion, snatches the money and the letter, and goes to* HELEN *who re-enters the room, reading it.* KATINA *closes the shutters.*]

PHILIP [*as* HELEN *reads*]: Dear Helen, I have arrived for the weekend. My bag is at the hotel near by. Sea, wind and saddle have taken their toll. My body stands exhausted at your door, awaiting sentence. If you really want to punish me for disobedience, in the time-honoured way of step-mothers in fairy-tales, you have only to send me back to Illinois without seeing me. But I'm hoping you'll find me a champion blackmailer as well as a top biographer.

[*Pause.*]

HELEN [*suddenly to* KATINA]: *Na perasi o kyrios.* (Show the gentleman in.)

[*The housekeeper protests.*]

Grigora! (I mean it.)

[KATINA *turns unwillingly to* PHILIP *and indicates curtly that he may proceed. He gives her a nervous smile and edges by the woman, who continues to watch balefully.*]

PHILIP [*approaching*]: *Kalispera.* That is correct, I hope?

HELEN [*coolly*]: You understand the Greek for good-evening, but not apparently the English for goodbye.

PHILIP: I had to come.

HELEN: Just for the weekend? From America?

PHILIP: Faint heart never won fair permission. I took the noon boat from Piraeus. I even survived the donkey. It was rougher than the sea . . . How many steps *are* there, actually?

HELEN: Three hundred and six.

PHILIP: I thought I was going to be pitched off at every turn . . . I guess people must have fallen over that cliff from time to time. [*Embarrassed.*] I'm sorry. That was clumsy.

HELEN: *Katina, tipot' allo. Efgaristo.* (That will be all. Thank you.)

[*Reluctantly* KATINA *goes. Throughout the ensuing* HELEN *retains a cold aloofness.* PHILIP *is very much on edge.*]

PHILIP [*indicating the basket of books*]: I see I was right about the professors.

HELEN: Oh, yes. Every week the boat delivers another little avalanche of self-recommendation. They're relentless, your countrymen.

PHILIP: I still think of myself as English.

[*Pause.*]

HELEN: How little you resemble him.

PHILIP: Really?

HELEN: You're so neat.

PHILIP: I believe I take after my mother.

HELEN: Do you see her?

PHILIP: She lives in Sheffield. That's a long way from Illinois.

HELEN: Her husband has a shop, I believe.

PHILIP: Camping equipment.

HELEN: Not exactly your world.

PHILIP: I guess that's why I left it.

[*The wind is heard faintly.*]

[*Indicating the terrace.*] I imagine you can see the famous view from that terrace. The cliffs of lava.

HELEN: Yes.

PHILIP: Could I go out and look?

HELEN: I'd rather you didn't. I'll give you a few minutes, only because you've come so far. I wouldn't waste them on views. Sit, if you like. [*Pause. He stays standing.*] Well?

PHILIP: Would you believe me if I said I knew every word Edward Damson wrote by heart – good, bad and indifferent? If I wasn't related, he'd still be an obsession. But he's not finally *there*. He's just a photo accepting awards in theatre magazines. I thought . . . if I could write his life . . .

HELEN: Yes?

PHILIP: He would become real for me.

[*Pause.*]

HELEN [*hostile*]: May I ask how long you have been in America?

PHILIP: Ten years. I went when I was eighteen.

HELEN: Long enough to catch the disease.

PHILIP: Excuse me?

HELEN: We all know that it's obligatory over there for

children of celebrated parents to write books abusing them after death. Setting the record straight, I believe it's called.

PHILIP: You're not saying that's what I want to do myself?

HELEN: Well, I doubt very much if you entertain feelings of overwhelming love for a man who totally abandoned you before you were born.

PHILIP: As a matter of fact, I've always felt relief that I wasn't raised by him.

HELEN: Really?

PHILIP: My stepfather is a peaceful man. Edward, I imagine, was hardly that.

HELEN: But he was well off. That is the point, isn't it? The royalties from his plays are considerable.

PHILIP: I don't understand. What point?

HELEN: You could have inherited a large income. One cannot help reflecting that a book about him – endorsed by me – would be a perfect way to redress that injustice. Make some money out of the situation, since he left you none.

PHILIP [*increasingly upset*]: That's awful . . . I'm sorry but that's really awful. You think I've come for revenge? Forgive me, but I think it may not be so good to live in *Greece* too long. I've always imagined people who live here have revenge on the brain.

HELEN [*startled*]: What do you mean by that?

PHILIP: If you knew what your husband meant to me – what he actually *is* to me – you couldn't possibly say that . . . Everything I am, everything I do, is because of him. His worship. *That's* my disease, if you like: worship of theatre. I got it from him, even though we never met. It was in me before I left England . . . [*Pause.*] . . . I never hassled him, you must know that. I did all my studies as far away from him as possible. Last year, when my dissertation was published, that was the first time I ever got in touch with him in my whole life! . . . Did he ever receive it, by the way? My book? He never acknowledged it.

HELEN: Just go on.

PHILIP: Listen, I'm a Mid-West academic who stands every day before students in a place totally removed from proper theatre. Expounding things to them completely remote from their own concerns: structure in Ibsen, symbolism in Chekhov, mythology in O'Neill – just because of *him*. Well, you're right, of course. I need money. Like every ex-graduate in America. You take out loans to buy education, you spend years paying them back. OK, I'm poor. I owe thousands of dollars. If I wanted to be cynical I could say he owes me for that. He saw to it I'd be poor for life! . . . So, if I ever earned anything out of a book on him, ten dollars or ten thousand, I'd actually deserve it. Well, at least a little . . . [*Nervously.*] That was a joke.

> [*Pause.*]

[*Stiffly.*] When you sent me that first letter, after he died, you said you'd found out about my existence and said you wanted to establish contact. I thought that meant you wanted to see me.

HELEN: I indicated quite firmly that I did not.

PHILIP: You mean that was to be our only contact? One letter?

HELEN: Contrary to what is believed in colleges, young man, playwrights do not exist to provide Professors of Drama with livelihoods.

PHILIP: That's a quotation from *him*. I recognize it. It's from one of his published diatribes against academics and commentators.

HELEN: So it is. The more intelligent opinions of husbands are liable to rub off on their wives. Now I think your time is up. I've really been quite generous, I think you'll agree.

> [*Pause.*]

PHILIP [*distressed*]: I used to think it was he who kept me away. I was wrong, wasn't I?

HELEN [*in sudden pain*]: Please! Just go!

7

[*In shock and anger* PHILIP *walks up to the shutters and deliberately opens them wide.*]

PHILIP: *His* view! His and yours alone. No one else to see it. No one else to see him, even a little – even after death.

HELEN [*low*]: Stop it, please.

PHILIP [*turning on her suddenly*]: I want my father. I want him. He's here! [*Raising his voice.*] I want him! Can't you understand? *What's the matter with you?*

[*Pause. She stares at him.*]

[*Recovering, very embarrassed.*] I'm sorry. I'm, I'm – I'm really sorry. I apologize. I've never – I'm not ever like this, ever . . .

[*The siren of a boat is heard. The wind fades.*]

HELEN [*suddenly*]: How long can you stay?

PHILIP: What?

HELEN: When do you have to return to America?

PHILIP: Two days. I've got classes on Tuesday.

HELEN: Come back in the morning. We'll speak then.

PHILIP [*bewildered*]: About what? . . . I don't understand.

HELEN [*simply*]: I agree, that's all.

PHILIP: Agree? . . .

HELEN: To your writing the book.

PHILIP: *You agree?*

HELEN: On one condition.

PHILIP: What? . . .

[*Pause.*]

HELEN [*standing by the great desk*]: Come here . . . Here.

[PHILIP *approaches the desk, warily.*]

This was his.

PHILIP: His desk?

HELEN: The only one he ever used.

PHILIP [*almost in a whisper*]: Oh, my God! He wrote all the plays on this?

HELEN: It's Russian. He bought it in Cambridge before I ever met him. Fifty pounds, I believe. He told me it once belonged to Rasputin.

PHILIP: Are you kidding?

HELEN: He said it should only be used therefore by Russian madmen.

PHILIP: Is that what *he* was? I knew his father was Russian.

HELEN: I want you to swear.

PHILIP: Swear?

HELEN: On this desk. To write his life.

PHILIP: That's all I *want*!

HELEN: Whatever happens.

PHILIP: What do you mean?

HELEN: Whatever you hear. No change of mind allowed. [*Pause.*] Well?

PHILIP [*uncomfortably*]: Well, yeah. All right.

HELEN: Put your hand on it . . . That was his altar, you see.
  [*He does so.*]

PHILIP [*laughing nervously*]: OK! I mean, I swear. Look, I don't get it. *Why?*
  [HELEN *closes the shutters.*]

HELEN: Just remember one thing. I didn't ask you here.

PHILIP: You sure didn't.

HELEN: You came yourself. You have to take the consequences of that.
  [*Pause.*]

PHILIP [*uncomfortably*]: Of course . . . I understand.
  [*Pause.*]

HELEN [*simply*]: No. You don't. [*Suddenly calling out.*] Katina! [*To him.*] Come back in the morning. Early.
  [KATINA *appears.*]

HELEN [*to* KATINA]: *Se parakalo, thikse tin porta.* [*To him.*] Katina will show you out.

KATINA [*beckoning to him*]: *Ella.*

PHILIP [*bewildered*]: You want me to go now?
  [*Abruptly* HELEN *leaves the room.*]

KATINA: *Ella.*

PHILIP [*calling after her*]: Have I done something to upset you?

KATINA: *Ella!*
PHILIP: *What do you want from me?*
KATINA [*insistently, tugging at him*]: *Ella! Ella!*
  [*She hustles him out. Wind. The light goes.*]

END OF SCENE ONE

ACT ONE

The next morning.

> [*Bright light. Wind and intermittent church bells. The shutters are open on to the terrace.* PHILIP *sits drinking coffee, a briefcase beside him.* HELEN *enters.*]

HELEN: Good morning.

PHILIP [*rising*]: Good morning.

HELEN [*nervously*]: Did you sleep?

PHILIP: Not much. Does this wind blow all the time?

HELEN: Most of it. At least you've had coffee.

PHILIP: Yes. Service with a scowl, I'm afraid. Your house-keeper disapproves of me.

HELEN: Disapproval is a fixed condition in all Greek peasant women over fifty. [*Indicating the desk.*] Now come and sit over here.

PHILIP [*smiling*]: At the altar?

HELEN: You want to make notes, I take it.

PHILIP: Yes, of course.

> [*He crosses and sits, taking from his briefcase an American pad of yellow paper, pencils and an electric pencil-sharpener.* HELEN *closes the shutters. The wind fades.*]

HELEN: What's that?

PHILIP: A toy from the New World. You see, I've come prepared.

> [*He demonstrates the sharpener with a pencil. It whizzes.* HELEN *stares at him.*]

HELEN: My friend, I'm sorry.

PHILIP [*perplexed*]: Sorry?

HELEN: For what will happen. To you.

PHILIP [*grinning*]: Are you trying to scare me?

HELEN: As sincerely as you may promise to forgive me now, you never will. I want you to know that.

PHILIP [*uneasily*]: As I say, I've come prepared.

    [*Pause.*]

HELEN: Then we begin. [*She sits.*] We actually started, he and I – I suppose symbolically – with violence.

PHILIP: You mean literally? Physically?

HELEN: Yes. The very first moment we met . . . Cambridge: summer 1975. I was living there, with my father.

PHILIP: He was a professor, wasn't he?

HELEN: An eminent one. I was hoping to follow in his footsteps. Somewhat haltingly, at twenty-five.

PHILIP [*surprised*]: You mean you were an academic?

HELEN: Post-graduate. Like you, I'd written a dissertation people liked. I was trying to work it up into a proper book: that meant spending most of my life in the library. Which is where I met Edward, and I mean really *met*. I was running out of the door and he was running in . . . *Ow!* It really hurt.

    [*The light changes abruptly.* HELEN *falls down, strewing books around her.* EDWARD *runs onstage and halts, looking across at her with open mouth. He is an unkempt man of twenty-eight in untidy clothes. When he speaks, the words tend to tumble out with massive energy, but also great relish in their phrasing.*]

Typically, *he* was furious.

EDWARD: Hell! What are you doing?

HELEN: What?

EDWARD: Women shouldn't run. They can't pull up.

    [*He picks up her books.*]

HELEN: He picked up my books rather than me. I always remember that.

    [*She picks herself up.*]

EDWARD [*examining the books*]: *Athena: Lore and Legend*, *Athena in the 'Agamemnon'*, *Athena and the Myth of Perseus* . . . Are you writing a book?

HELEN [*hostile*]: I could be.

EDWARD: On the Goddess Athena?

HELEN: Well, it looks like it, doesn't it?

EDWARD: I haven't seen you before. Do you live here?

HELEN [*taking the books back abruptly*]: My father is Professor of Greek, as a matter of fact.

EDWARD: Ah, ha! Jarvis!

HELEN: You know him?

EDWARD: Everyone knows him. He's also President of the Peace League, or whatever it's called.

HELEN: Not President, or anything like.

EDWARD: Well, a big noise in it, anyway. A major Turn-the-Other-Cheeker. Are you too?

HELEN [*irritated*]: What?

EDWARD: A pacifist. A Peace-At-Any-Pricer?

HELEN: I support his views, if that's any of your business. Now, goodbye.

EDWARD: Actually I could a tale unfold about your dad.

HELEN: What do you mean?

EDWARD: You'll have to come home to hear it. You need a drink, anyway.

HELEN: Do I?

EDWARD: Pepper vodka. Infallible after shock.

HELEN: I think not, thank you.

EDWARD: Oh, come on! You may have a broken rib.

HELEN: No, thank you all the same.

PHILIP: But you went?

HELEN [*to* PHILIP]: Yes. To a tiny house in Malcolm Street. A stifling little room – gas fire, papers everywhere. An unmade bed and this desk taking up most of the room.

[*Light change as they enter it: warmer.*]

EDWARD: My sanctum! Only the glinting admitted.

HELEN: Glinting?

EDWARD: People who catch the light.

HELEN: Well, that excludes me.

EDWARD: I think not, as you would say. Here.

[*He picks up two china mugs.*]

HELEN [*to* PHILIP]: It was incomprehensible, actually. I wasn't the sort to be borne off. Or fed firewater in a dirty tooth-mug.

[*She chokes on the vodka.*]

EDWARD: You hate it?

HELEN [*bravely*]: No, it's stimulating . . . Who lives here?

EDWARD: The United Nations. Top floor: Nigerian princess studying history. Middle: pallid biochemist from Tamworth. Ground: enormous economist from Kansas, and me: Russian–Welsh.

HELEN: Really?

EDWARD: My dad is a refugee from Moscow. Retired from Her Majesty's Post Office. Now just sits in the basement telling his dog stories of the Romanovs. Mother's the Welsh. Baptist, compulsively long-suffering. That's her predominant emotion: Putting-Up-with-Things. She rents rooms to students. I help with the cleaning. Father disdains such work.

HELEN: Because he's an aristocrat?

EDWARD: Because *his* leading emotion is disdain. He is actually the son of a storekeeper.

HELEN: And what do you do, apart from the cleaning? You're not a student.

EDWARD: At twenty-eight? Of course not.

PHILIP [*startled*]: He was twenty-eight? That's my age! Exactly what I am now.

HELEN: Well, you can be satisfied in having achieved rather more than he had.

EDWARD: I'm a wastrel. Ask around. Most of Cambridge disapproves of me. Led by your father.

HELEN: What do you mean?

EDWARD: He actually ordered me out of one of his lectures. I'd interrupted him to correct a mistake he'd made.

HELEN: You didn't?

EDWARD: He was impossibly prissy about it. It didn't help that I'd gate-crashed.

HELEN: Do you often do that?

EDWARD: Certainly. All the best people are here, speaking. Strict honesty forbids me to include your father in that category.

HELEN: Thank you.

EDWARD: No, but he is *totally* without glint! I heard enough of his lecture on the *Agamemnon* to realize that in ten minutes. And he took no account whatever of the rightness of Clytemnestra chopping up her husband in that bath.

HELEN: *Rightness?*

EDWARD: Certainly. It was an absolutely *right* thing to do. You don't agree?

HELEN: Of course I don't. Agamemnon was completely helpless. In a *bath*, for God's sake!

EDWARD: Well, so was his daughter when he sacrificed her on an altar. His wife simply cleaned the slate. Sacrifice for sacrifice . . . That's what bloodshed can do – clean things.

HELEN: You don't believe that?

EDWARD: Profoundly. So did the Greeks. If you don't understand that, you don't understand *them*. Have you ever been there? To Greece?

HELEN: Endlessly. My parents took me every summer. I actually detested it.

EDWARD: You did?

HELEN: Oh, yes. It was always so dusty and remorseless. And all those stones never interested me at all.

EDWARD: That's absurd. You must go back there at once! That place can tell you who you are. It did me.

HELEN: Really? And who *are* you?

EDWARD: A playwright. The world's most indispensable job.

HELEN: Indispensable?

EDWARD: Certainly.

HELEN: How many plays have you written?

EDWARD: Fifty. The climactic scenes, anyway. There's no point in writing the rest – they're never going to be produced. People prefer the shrivelled stuff – reflections of their own shrivelled lives.

PHILIP [*laughing*]: Was he as dogmatic as that even then?

HELEN [*to* PHILIP]: I think that was what hooked me – his vehemence. Relentless as it was!

EDWARD: Here we're all so oblique. We're sick from *oblique*. Bloody deballed, self-conscious, your-serve-my-serve English Oblique! ... There's nothing oblique about Agamemnon lying cut up in that bath. That's drama – clear and clean. Pure revenge, which means pure justice.

HELEN: Revenge? That's not justice.

EDWARD: That's exactly what it is! The best and truest. Look at *Hamlet*. What d'you think that's about? 'Revenge my foul and most unnatural murder!' – that's all. Will you *clean* the world or leave it dirty? The only mistake Shake-speare makes is to forget the ghost at the end. We should actually see it stalking away, satisfied at last, daubing the blood of Claudius on its spectral cheeks.

PHILIP: Well, that's a point, anyway! The ghost *is* forgotten.

HELEN [*to* PHILIP]: So it should be! The play's more *advanced* than that! [*To* EDWARD.] Hamlet reaches a point where he says, 'Let be.' That means going beyond the *need* for revenge. That's why it's the most advanced play ever written. Because it took a naturally blood-thirsty audience to that same point!

EDWARD: And what's so advanced about that? Just giving up with a shrug – as if you never really cared about the wrong in the first place? *Avoidance*, that's all that is! ... There's

16

only one real moral imperative: don't piss on true rage – it can be the fire of sanity.

PHILIP [*noting it down*]: Good phrase!

EDWARD: I told you: sometimes you have to clean yourself with blood.

HELEN: I don't know what that means. If you show violence to a violent man –

EDWARD [*impatiently*]: You turn into him yourself. Yes, yes, I've heard. That's your father talking.

HELEN [*tightly*]: I must go.

EDWARD: Tell me first: if a thug killed your dad tonight – brutally and deliberately – wouldn't you wish him killed in return? In your deepest heart?

HELEN: Possibly – But it would be wrong.

EDWARD: There speaks the voice of our healthy, happy society.

HELEN: Excuse me!

EDWARD [*seriously*]: I tell you, if it was someone *I* loved who was killed, I would need to honour life by killing the killer. Preferably with my own hand.

HELEN: And you call that honouring?

EDWARD [*hard*]: So should you – or you honour nothing.

HELEN: Thanks for the vodka. Not my drink, I'm afraid.

[*She makes to go.*]

EDWARD: Don't leave!

HELEN [*angry*]: I don't need any more of this! Really!

EDWARD: Please! [*He falls impulsively on his knees.*] Look, I'm excessive. I'm extreme. I can't stop! Extreme Edward, it's my nickname! It'll be on my tombstone: HERE LIES EDWARD DAMSON WHO LIVED HIS WHOLE LIFE *in extremis*! . . . Please stay.

HELEN: Is that your name – Damson?

EDWARD: Sharp and purple, like my dialogue. What's yours?

HELEN: Helen.

EDWARD: You have a mother?

HELEN: She died four years ago.

EDWARD: I bet she was a professor too.

HELEN: How can you tell?

EDWARD: Because you're steeped in it. It's obvious.

HELEN: It is?

EDWARD: You simply shine with learning. Rays of erudition surround you like a nimbus!

HELEN: Yes? Well, I must take them away with me now. I've got a supervision in twenty minutes.

EDWARD: You supervise? At your age?

HELEN: Well, it pays a little.

EDWARD: Wonderful! A truly learned girl! May we meet tomorrow?

HELEN: No, I'm sorry. I'm working all day.

EDWARD: You really keep your nose jammed to the grindstone, don't you?

HELEN: It mightn't be a bad idea if you did the same. Bye.
    [*She walks away from him.*]

EDWARD [*calling after her*]: Right! You're right, you see? You *know* me! . . . What's going to happen to me, learned girl?
    [*She sits at the desk. Light change to indicate her house.*]

HELEN: The next day as I sat down to work at home, I thought to myself, That's that. I shan't see *him* again! . . . And then I realized I'd left all those books behind. And almost at the same moment . . .
    [*Door knock.* EDWARD *presents himself, holding the books.*]

EDWARD: Here! I've read them all.

HELEN: I don't believe you.

EDWARD: The main bits, anyway. The bits that glinted.

HELEN [*briskly*]: Well, that's very industrious. And now you must go. My father will be back from his lecture and it's our sharing-hour – noon to one. Thanks for these.

EDWARD [*smiling*]: Athena was obviously the most aggressive of all the Gods.

HELEN: That's not true.

EDWARD: Do you know how she was *born?* She sprang from the head of Zeus fully armed!

HELEN: To keep order. That was her chief function: keep man temperate.

EDWARD: *Temperate?* The first sounds out of her mouth were war-cries! The sun was so shocked it just stood still in the sky.

HELEN: *Warning* cries, not war. All her most famous actions are about *restraint.* Like the famous bridle she put on Pegasus, the winged horse. It's obviously a parable about the need to control your spirit, so it doesn't run you into chaos.

EDWARD: Well, in this country restraint is the ultimate avoidance-word! Restraint–Taste–Moderation: they're all niminy-wiminy qualities in the end, prized most by professors – I bet your dad uses them all the time.

HELEN: You know absolutely nothing about my father, so stop right there!

EDWARD: I know he throws deserving students out of lectures, and turns Aeschylus into anaesthesia. Isn't that enough?

[PROFESSOR JARVIS *enters, austere and middle-aged.*]

Ah, good morning, sir. We were just talking about Athena. I was saying she is the most aggressive female in Greek mythology. Would you agree?

JARVIS [*drily*]: Actually her profoundest achievement was to present mankind with the olive. As oil, a symbol of domesticity. In branch, a symbol of peace.

EDWARD: Ah.

JARVIS: Now, if you will excuse us.

[*Pause.*]

EDWARD [*abruptly to* HELEN]: I'll see you.

[*He moves away, out of the light.*]

HELEN: He's actually quite interesting when you know him.

19

JARVIS: Dear one, do you remember I told you I had to ask someone to leave a lecture? And last month a man was ejected from a League meeting because he kept shouting at the speakers? They were both him.

HELEN: Are you sure?

JARVIS: It's not a face one forgets . . .

HELEN: No.

JARVIS: Frankly, it's alarming to me. It emits a kind of message.

HELEN: Really?

JARVIS: Unalterable scorn for everything we believe in.

HELEN: You've always said there's no such person as an unalterable enemy.

JARVIS: Then let's just admit I haven't the inclination to try and alter Mr Damson. If that's his real name.

HELEN: What do you mean?

JARVIS: Well, doesn't it sound made up to you?

HELEN: No!

JARVIS: This is a person, one senses, who brings pain. Please, dearest. I have no right to ask, but I would be really happy if you didn't see him again.

HELEN: All right. I will try not to.

JARVIS: Thank you. Dear one.

[*He kisses her gratefully.*]

PHILIP: And did you? . . .

HELEN: I went back to Malcolm Street the same week. And met *his* father.

[*She joins* EDWARD *at the desk.* MR DAMSINSKI, *Edward's Russian father, shuffles in, in slippers.* EDWARD *hastily conceals the bottle.*]

DAMSINSKI [*to* HELEN]: Damsinski! . . . I salute you, Mademoiselle.

HELEN: [*looking at* EDWARD, *amused*] Damsinski?

DAMSINSKI: Why not? A good honourable name. It's only my son who is ashamed of it.

EDWARD: It has nothing to do with shame. I want my own name, not anybody else's. Damson is the right one for me. Your damn son.

DAMSINSKI: Ha, ha! Self-crowned, like Napoleon! Magnificent arrogance! I salute it! – Do you have vodka with you?

EDWARD: No.

DAMSINSKI: Please, Teddy. That's not kind. Your mother smashed my bottle this morning. Just threw it down into the backyard. A whole big bottle, the real Macoysky. Smish-smesh, just like that!

EDWARD: Why?

DAMSINSKI: Because I refuse to make the bed for that black girl upstairs! It is really too much. A person of my standing to make the bed of a little nigsky who calls herself princess! What princess? From Boola-Boola?

EDWARD [*embarrassed*]: Please!

DAMSINSKI: And because of that, no vodka all day. Smish-smesh! [*To* HELEN.] Life here is unbearable.

HELEN: I'm sorry.

EDWARD [*producing a bottle*]: Here. Take it, dammit. I had reserved this for myself.

DAMSINSKI [*taking it*]: The proper stuff too. Absolute real Macoysky! You are a true saint. [*To* HELEN.] He is, I have to admit it, in spite he likes nigskys. He likes all of them you know: nogskys, wogskys, pigskys and pogskys! I can't stand *any*. They're all dangerous. They're going to smash the world soon, and no one can see it. Smish-smesh.

EDWARD: *Oh, for God's sake!* She doesn't want to hear this. And neither do I.

DAMSINSKI: All right, I'll go away. A prophet is never honoured in his own adopted country. That's my joke. I will go down to my kennel with my poor Anastasia. She shares my life – my sorrows and my vodka. Only dog in Cambridge to drink pepper vodka. That's some style, ha? . . . Mademoiselle.

[*He bows to* HELEN *and shuffles out.*]

HELEN: Fathers can be difficult.

EDWARD: Well, you tell yours from me I'm the least irresponsible man he will ever meet! Just because I can't stand his crowd of pacifist Give-Uppers and Lie-Downers doesn't make me irresponsible. He's got his faith and I've got mine – and he should respect mine more because it happens to be infinitely realer than his.

HELEN: Oh, yes? And what is that?

EDWARD: The theatre, of course. The only religion that can never die . . . It's quiescent now, like an old fire fallen in on itself, barely smouldering. But at its height, centuries ago here in England just as much as Greece, the theatre gave us faith and True Astonishment – as religion is supposed to do. The playwright set up his play like Athena's shield: a great shining surface in which you can see all truth by reflection! The audience assembled before it, and peered into it together, in communion. They saw themselves enlarged – made legendary as well as particular, in all their glory and ghastliness. It faced them with towering shapes of their most intense and terrible desires. Undeniable pictures, formed of blazing words. They came away astounded. Scared. Exalted. Seeing themselves, perhaps for the first time, and their world – which they'd always thought ordinary – lit with the fire of *transformation*! . . . As they walked home, they'd suddenly really *see* the 'dragon-wing of night o'erspread the earth'! And inside themselves the glint of their own true beings. Theatre was an *illuminant*, sacred and indispensable. What is it now? Rows of seats for people to sit with folded arms. People who have forgotten their needs.

[*Pause.*]

I tell you, one day, stirred by new priests, that fire will blaze again. Then watch out!

[*Pause.*]

[*Shyly.*] And one of those priests could be me.

[*He stares at her. She stares back.*]

EDWARD: You find me absurd?

HELEN: No.

[*Slowly he kisses her.*]

EDWARD [*gravely*]: It's all that matters to me.

[*A faint music. He rises. She stays seated. Light change.*]

HELEN [*to* PHILIP]: And then he pulled the coverlet off the bed and spread it on the floor, by the gas fire.

[EDWARD *bends forward as if leaning over her, then lies down.*]

EDWARD [*tenderly*]: My learned girl.

HELEN: He was Russian, all right. Dusk was falling and the street-lamp sprang on outside, making shadows on his face, and I saw a Tartar. A hood-eyed Russian savage. The eyes concentrated in a way I'd never seen. Like a student learning a theorem . . . Each time we made love after that he looked the same.

PHILIP [*embarrassed*]: Please!

HELEN: What?

PHILIP: You don't have to tell me this.

HELEN: We said 'everything'.

PHILIP: All the same . . .

[*He falls silent.* EDWARD *lies full length, as if beside her on the coverlet.*]

HELEN: We made love with elaborate tenderness, always. Surprising, because he wasn't a tender man. Especially then – locked up in a state of fear and unachievement.

[*She kneels beside him.*]

I let him out. That's my one claim. It's nothing special. That's what we women are good at – delivering   But first, he had to deliver me.

[EDWARD *reaches out his hand to her.*]

I'd had lovers, a few, but yet not. In a real way I was still virgin. That Sunday afternoon Edward touched me and the world changed irreversibly.

[EDWARD *leaves the stage as* JARVIS *comes in and sits at the desk. She rises and moves to him. Faint music continues.*]

As I walked home, objects seemed insistently clear. Our door knocker in the shape of a fish, with smears of Brasso on its head . . . At dinner father sat chewing a cutlet. I saw the wrinkles round his mouth. Poor, difficult, idealistic man. No wife – and soon perhaps no daughter. And then and there 'soon' became 'now'. The fish jumped on the door, and it was all over for him.

[*The knocker bangs. Light change. Music breaks off.* EDWARD *rushes in.*]

JARVIS: Who on earth's that?

HELEN: All our good times – all our chess games and chuckles, reading together, our little rituals – going, going, *gone!*

[*Knocker sounds again.*]

EDWARD [*calling roughly*]: Helen!

HELEN [*to* JARVIS]: I'll get it.

[*She turns to* EDWARD.]

EDWARD: 'Tis I – Hamlet, the Dane!

HELEN [*to* PHILIP]: Obviously drunk, on the doorstep. [*To* EDWARD.] It's so late!

EDWARD: I'm going to Greece. Will you come with me?

HELEN [*lowered voice*]: When?

EDWARD: This week. I've just decided.

HELEN: I couldn't.

EDWARD: Why not?

HELEN: For one thing, I can't afford it. I haven't that kind of money.

EDWARD: Greece is the cheapest place on earth. You can see all of it for fifty pounds: every single island worth your scrutiny. Kos. Kiss. Clitoris. The lot.

HELEN: Sssssh!

EDWARD: I'm going in to see him.

HELEN: What for? . . .

[*He brushes past her.*]

[*In panic*]: Edward!

EDWARD [*turning*]: That's done it. You've called me by my name.

[*He moves to* JARVIS. *She stands still.*]

HELEN: Oh, God!

EDWARD: I would like a word, sir, please. About Helen.

JARVIS: Yes?

HELEN [*to* PHILIP]: I stood outside, eavesdropping. Like a Victorian maiden.

EDWARD: I have asked her to travel with me to the Aegean Sea. She's absolutely ready for it. Unfortunately she lacks the appropriate money. Also, no doubt, the effrontery, which I have – I'm told in deplorable measure – to ask you for it. I have therefore undertaken this delicate embassy on her behalf. I can of course provide entirely for my own needs.

JARVIS: Mr Damson, I see no point in mincing words. I consider you a less than desirable companion for my daughter.

EDWARD: What a dreadful description. Imagine having that inscribed on your tombstone: HE WAS LESS THAN DESIRABLE!

JARVIS: I am prepared to admit you may possess qualities I do not perceive. I am afraid I can only speak – like all of us – as I find. Helen is an exceptional girl. She has ahead of her a brilliant future. I would not wish her to spend any part of her life with those who would waste it.

EDWARD [*agitated*]: What?!

JARVIS: This house does not welcome idleness, Mr Damson, which is what I see in you. An old pose: idleness masquerading as creative fallow.

EDWARD: That is shameful.

JARVIS: I'm sorry if that is too blunt.

EDWARD: You have no right, you have absolutely no right,

to say that of me! Waste! . . . I do not *waste* people! Ever!
. . . Others – For example, *you*! You waste, entirely.

JARVIS: What do you say?

EDWARD: The students in your care – attending your lectures
on the Classics – *they* are being wasted, every boring hour
they hear you! Their enthusiasm, their hunger for revelation! [*Working himself up.*] I heard those dreary, dead ten
minutes before you threw me out. I would be ashamed,
actually *ashamed*, to make the ancient world as dead as that!

JARVIS: Yes, well. Would you please leave now? I think we've
said everything, Mr Damson – or whatever your real name is!

EDWARD: Real? That *is* my real name! What's yours? . . .
Parvus! Yes, *Parvus*. Parvus-Jarvis: Small-change man! How
about *that*?

[*He laughs at his own joke.* HELEN *bursts into the scene.*]

HELEN: Edward, stop it! . . . How *can* you?

EDWARD [*crying out*]: Damson! I am Damson! – Remember
it! . . . The world's going to! . . . Dam–dam–Damson!

[*He rushes away upstage, past* HELEN. *Father and daughter
stand rigid.*]

HELEN [*to* PHILIP]: The door banged. Father and I just
stood. In that silence our partnership ended. And then
suddenly I ran out of the house. After him. All the way
across the city. Right into his room!

[*She rushes breathless at him.*]

[*To* EDWARD]: Damn *you*! . . . Damn *you*! [*He turns
away.*] You are the most despicable man I've ever met! . . .
Actually, I think you're mad. You're not just rude – this
place is full of arrogant, rude men – you're really hateful!

[*She bursts into tears. He turns round, in pain.*]

EDWARD: Yes! . . . Yes! Yes! I know! . . . I can't stop it. I
can't help myself! It's why we're going to Greece. Greece
cures madness.

HELEN: We? . . . Do you really think I'm going anywhere
with *you*?

EDWARD: You've got to!

HELEN: Got?

EDWARD: You must! You have to! [*Sticking out his tongue.*] Look! – this thing – look! It has to be tamed! Made to praise, not rave all day! It's a praising instrument. I can't spend my life with *this*!

HELEN: Oh, *stop* it! Stop *posing*!

EDWARD: No, I'm mad. You've got it right. Only you can cure me!

HELEN: Goodbye, Edward.

EDWARD: For Christ's sake! [*He grabs her.*] Understand it! If you don't come with me, I'll never go there. I'll never *see* Greece. Ever!

HELEN: What are you talking about? You've seen it already!

EDWARD: No!

HELEN: But you *told* me!

[*Pause.*]

EDWARD [*sheepishly*]: From a bus, that's all. Two weeks on a package tour, with a girl. It was a lark to her. She wasn't remotely interested in Greece.

HELEN: Just in you?

EDWARD: And I in her. For the two weeks.

PHILIP [*understanding*]: Of course! . . .

EDWARD: Alas for us both.

PHILIP: It was my mother, wasn't it? She told me once. One of her few mentions of him, ever. 'We had two weeks together in a bus,' she said.

HELEN: Yes.

EDWARD: A secretary in one of the colleges here. A prim little girl . . . Not exactly tempestuous romance. But prim can excite. It's what first got me with *you*.

[*Pause.* HELEN *stares at him.*]

PHILIP: Didn't he mention me at all?

HELEN [*to* PHILIP]: I wrote you. You were a surprise for much later.

PHILIP: All this was in '75 . . . I was already ten.

HELEN [*to* EDWARD]: Where is she now?

EDWARD: A small town near here.

PHILIP: Royston. A flat over a service garage. Where I was brought up.

HELEN: How much money do you actually have?

EDWARD: How much d'you think? I get fifteen pounds a week from my mother, plus room and board. And I review books for magazines. As many as I can get.

HELEN: You take money from your mother?

EDWARD: I earn it. I clean students' rooms. That's hard work. They're pigs. What else would you have me do? Slave for the Post Office like my dad? I've inherited unemployability. Isn't it obvious? [*Intimately.*] Please, Learned, come with me. Be my saviour. We can do it together.

[*He kisses her, passionately, and she surrenders. The light changes during the following, becoming warmer. The faintest Greek music starts presently.*]

PHILIP: So you went?

HELEN [*to* PHILIP]: The next day . . . I was a coward, I left a note when father was lecturing – FORGIVE ME. BACK IN A FORTNIGHT – knowing it was a lie . . . Incredibly, in six visits as a child, I'd never seen it. Suddenly it was all there – all calling to me, immense and wonderful. The Isles of Greece! Those countless boats bobbing between them – cargo boats, fishing boats and dolphins. That actually happened once, dolphins keeping us company! And the light – that light, yes – the *glint* if you like, so uncompromising. No wonder he loved it. It was like *him*.

EDWARD [*still holding her*]: Learned! Brave and learned!

HELEN: Slowly I saw his confidence begin, right there in the sunshine! The true thing . . . Incredible to think it had to do with me! I'd never inspired that in anyone . . . I kept thinking, how can he want to be with *me*?

[*He kisses her hands.*]

That was the wonder, you see. His *need*. I had never been needed. Depended on, yes – not needed.

[*He kneels and kisses her belly.*]

PHILIP: Tell me, if you had known about me then, would you have gone with him? I mean, that he had an adolescent son living a few miles away.

HELEN: It wouldn't have mattered a scrap . . . I'm sorry.

[*Music breaks off abruptly.*]

PHILIP: Why apologize? It meant nothing to him, after all. When did he actually tell you about me? Five years later? Ten?

HELEN: In order, Philip. Let's just stay now in Greece – the terrible bright place.

[*Light change.* EDWARD *rises.*]

We were at Mycenae. We'd visited the famous Lion Gate under which Agamemnon passed to his murder in that bath. We were staying in an awful little hotel by the ruins. The cheapest room we could find.

[EDWARD *takes off his shirt.*]

EDWARD: The last time I came here we went to a taverna. They did that irritating dance from *Zorba the Greek*. [*Singing.*] Doopy-doopy-doo! . . . I want to erase that memory. I could show you Clytemnestra's Stamp. That would do it.

HELEN: What on earth's that?

EDWARD: You should know. She did it right after she'd hacked up her husband. She danced it around the ghost as it rose from the soil of the bath-house. First she got priestesses to wash her body in *lustration*: to show him how pure she felt. Then she did a Dance of Rightful Stamping. It's in the *Iliad*.

HELEN: I don't remember that.

EDWARD: Homer records all the steps in minute detail. I studied them.

HELEN: What Book?

EDWARD: How should I know? Do you want to see it or not?

HELEN: You're making this up, aren't you?

EDWARD: I only make up truths.

HELEN: Whatever that means.

EDWARD: Ask any artist.

HELEN: I want to know what Book of the *Iliad*, please.

EDWARD: Look, pedant! Either you want to see the dance or you don't. Yes or no?

HELEN: No.

EDWARD: Very well.

HELEN: Well, yes, of course! . . . Of course!

EDWARD: All right. Give me a moment to prepare. It is an extremely difficult thing to perform. It was intended to defy the spirit of a raging Greek warrior. A man who should have atoned for his crime and never did.

[*He leaves the stage.*]

HELEN [*to* PHILIP]: In the corner of our room was a tiny shower. Your father shed his clothes, just where he stood, stepped into it, turned on the water, then called to me.

[*The sound of the shower is heard.*]

EDWARD [*calling from offstage*]: First you must cleanse me. Physically. As if you are wiping all stain from me. Then salute my purity with a bow.

HELEN: He was standing there naked, holding a cube of soap. One of those large cubes they make in Greece, with a design of olives embossed into it. Olive-oil soap . . .

[*She stops in sudden distress.*]

PHILIP [*softly*]: Yes?

HELEN: He raised his arms and I soaped him all over. He loved it. It made him glisten . . . He told me to sit like an audience, then he stepped out from behind the curtain. The sun was setting through the window, scorching red. [*In difficulty.*] And he danced.

[EDWARD *runs in, wearing a large white towel pulled up*

over his head to suggest a woman. He stands stock still, arms upraised. HELEN *bows to him. A menacing music starts. Suddenly* EDWARD *emits a high falsetto scream − a female ululation − and begins to stamp. Rhythmically he swings an invisible axe down on an invisible husband, making wild animal cries of increasing intensity.* HELEN *watches in fascination as his dance grows wilder and the light redder and redder. Finally, as he approaches her with extended hands, it appears to stain his chest and towel. The undertow of sound boils up beneath and with a gasp of horror* HELEN *turns away from the scene. It stops abruptly.* EDWARD *hurries from the stage and the light changes back.*]

PHILIP: Are you all right? . . . Helen?

[*Abruptly she leaves the room. She is shaking.*]

[*Calling after her.*] He danced, yes – so? . . . Helen!

[*He makes to follow her. Suddenly* KATINA *is standing in the same place in the doorway, barring his way.*]

KATINA [*harshly*]: *I kyria leyhi na fighete!* (The mistress says Go!)

PHILIP: I don't understand.

KATINA [*putting up six fingers*]: *Boris na erthis etho, stis exi!* (You may come back here at six.) *Exi! Exi!*

PHILIP: I must return at six? Six o'clock?

KATINA: *Tora fighe!* (Now go!) *Fighe! . . . Fighe!*

[*She points imperiously. Intimidated, he goes out. The light fades. From offstage we hear the sound of* HELEN *crying. A faint wind.*]

END OF ACT ONE

ACT TWO

Later that afternoon.

[*Bells ringing faintly.* PHILIP *sits at the desk, drinking a cup of tea, watched by* HELEN *and her scowling house-keeper.*]

PHILIP [*drinking*]: Good. I guess something atavistic in me makes me love English tea. The tannin must get into the genes. [*To* KATINA.] *Efgaristo.*
[*She shrugs.*]

HELEN [*to her*]: *Tora se parakalo mi mas enohlis.* (Now please don't disturb us.)
[KATINA *grunts and goes out.*]

PHILIP: I owe you an apology. I called you Helen this morning. I didn't mean to be so familiar.

HELEN: It is for me to apologize. You have only two days, and I waste the better part of one not appearing. Have you passed a bearable day?

PHILIP: I explored the island a little. It's rather austere.

HELEN: Grim would be nearer.

PHILIP: Look — if you're finding this really impossible — I'll understand. With extreme reluctance, of course.

HELEN [*coldly*]: We are committed, as I remember. We made a bargain.

PHILIP: All the same —

HELEN: So we go on.

PHILIP [*surprised*]: OK, you'll get no argument from me . . .

HELEN: We were in Greece. Now we return to England. To our marriage. And our glamorous life together.

PHILIP: When was your wedding?

HELEN: As soon as we returned.

> [*Light change.* EDWARD *enters sulkily.* PHILIP *sharpens his pencils.*]

HELEN: My father, of course, did not attend. It was the only time I met his mother. She didn't like me.

EDWARD: She has forgotten how to like. Poor woman, she was brought up to believe that work has to be unpleasant or it isn't real work. Theatre is top of her list of what's frivolous . . . Frankly, I don't know why we've come back to this country at all.

HELEN: Because this is where it counts, and you know it.

EDWARD: Balls! You just talk such real balls, Learned!

> [*He seats himself at the marble-topped desk where* PHILIP *sits, spreads his paper all over it, and starts to write impetuously, in blue ink. As he works, he seems to push his son and his notebook progressively further to one small part of the desk.*]

HELEN [*to* PHILIP]: But I was right. If you want to write plays, you can't do that in Greece. The Greeks believe that theatre stopped with Euripides.

> [PHILIP *laughs.*]

I can't say it was easy for him. A dingy flat above a fish and chip shop in Kilburn.

> [*Light change to indicate their home.*]

EDWARD: Hell on earth, English style! [*To* HELEN.] This room must be the nastiest in London.

HELEN: It's all we can afford.

EDWARD: *I* can't afford it. I'll be dead in six months, staying here. Or at least doused. Any flicker of flame put out Killburn: oh, yes!

> [*He goes on writing.*]

HELEN [*to* PHILIP]: I'd found a job to support us. A travel agency. Sixty-five pounds a week, which in those days was not bad.

EDWARD: Totally unworthy of you! If you want to settle for Not Bad, you're sunk. Not Bad killed more people than Appalling . . . You should be writing about Athena, not sending typists on coach trips to Delphi!

HELEN: In the long run I suspect I'm doing much more good, working at that!

EDWARD: It's just blackmail, that's all. Emotional blackmail on a monumental scale.

HELEN: Then yield to it. Write something.

EDWARD [*picking up the piece of paper scribbled over in blue ink*]: Well, what do you think this is – *wanking*?

[*He tears it up.*]

HELEN [*protesting*]: What *was* that?

EDWARD: Why don't we go to America? It's no good here any more. It's rotting – you can smell! A stink stronger than those chips coming up the stairs.

HELEN: You'd hate America more. I know that.

EDWARD: Oh, no, I wouldn't! America's got glint. Ours has gone for good. There's nothing here now but drizzle, emotional and physical. Look at it out there – liquefied defeat.

HELEN: Do you know what you sound like? One of those whining characters you despise on the stage – simply attacking things all day.

[*Pause.*]

EDWARD [*suddenly laughing*]: Good! You are absolutely right! I am becoming a bore. Here please, Grave and Learned, your corrective lips!

[*They kiss.*]

HELEN [*to* PHILIP]: Understand, I never regretted for one day putting my life with his. We counted once, about that time, we'd made love every day for four months . . . Does that embarrass you?

PHILIP [*embarrassed*]: Of course not! . . .

HELEN: And we went to the theatre in the same way – night

after night! Up in the gods for the first act, then down for the second, wherever we spied empty seats . . . Of course, it was Shakespeare we saw most.

EDWARD [*throwing down his pen and stretching out his arms to her*]: Time 'scants us with a single famish'd kiss, distasted with the salt of broken tears'. Writing that line justifies human evolution.

HELEN [*lightly*]: Yes, well, what are *you* writing?

EDWARD: Nothing.

[*He tears up the paper in front of him.*]

HELEN [*protesting*]: Edward!

[*He tears up another.*]

Stop it!

EDWARD: The perfect written thing is the nearest man gets to immortality. The approximate thing dismisses him . . . And if you are only capable of the latter, why start?

HELEN: Well, you never actually *do* – do you?

EDWARD: That's all I *ever* do. I start a new play every day.

HELEN: I know. That's the trouble.

EDWARD: What do you mean by that?

HELEN: Well, it's obvious. All start, no finish.

EDWARD: Thank you.

HELEN: It's true.

EDWARD: Can't you understand? – I'm suffering from a sacred affliction. Only divinely favoured people know about it. Every morning in the head ten brilliantly coloured ideas end up making one perfect white. It's a kind of active paralysis. And it's absolutely incurable, so you'd better get used to it.

HELEN: It can't be.

EDWARD: Fifty plays started and abandoned? Of course it is.

HELEN: Rubbish. It's simply –

EDWARD: What?

HELEN: Well, not *simply*, exactly –

EDWARD: What?

HELEN: Well, a kind of fear, I suppose.

EDWARD: Of what?

HELEN: I don't know. I don't want to be glib.

EDWARD: You said 'fear': you must have something in mind.

HELEN: Well, of being judged, I imagine.

EDWARD: What are you saying?

HELEN: I don't know . . . Forget it.

EDWARD: Judged. What do you mean – judged?

HELEN: Well, if one doesn't ever finish anything one can't ever be valued, can one?

EDWARD: Well, that's just silly.

HELEN: Is it?

EDWARD: That's just the stupidest thing I ever heard. No, actually, it's really nasty. That's about as nasty as I've ever heard you get.

HELEN: Well, I'm sorry. I didn't intend – You know I didn't intend –

EDWARD [*exploding*]: No! It's all right. Fine! Fine! . . . Just cut them off, why don't you? [*Grabbing his testicles.*] It's what you want to do, isn't it? . . . I presume that's what you finally want to do!

HELEN: Edward –

EDWARD: *Damn you! . . . Damn you to hell!*

[*A dreadful silence. He moves violently away from her. Then, in panic, he rushes back and falls abruptly at her feet, grabbing her waist in supplication. She takes his head in her hands.*]

HELEN [*to* PHILIP]: My one fear was that his need for me would run out.

PHILIP: Yes.

HELEN: My one prayer, that he would actually *complete* a piece of work. One big, worked-out epic play.

PHILIP: To confound your father, among other things.

HELEN: Of course.

[*The light changes.* JARVIS *and* DAMSINSKI *both enter and sit in separate areas.* HELEN *and* EDWARD *go to their respective parents.*]

JARVIS [*to* HELEN]: Does he work at *all*?

HELEN: He writes plays.

JARVIS: I mean, to support you.

HELEN: They will in time.

JARVIS: Really?

DAMSINSKI: Your mother is closing down. No more students. Says she can't do it any more. What fun it's going to be now, with just her and me.

JARVIS [*to* HELEN]: I'm selling the house. There's no point in keeping it for one person.

HELEN: Don't be bitter, please. There was always the possibility I would have met somebody. You must have realized that.

JARVIS [*ironic*]: Somebody!

DAMSINSKI: You haven't brought any vodka, have you? I've got absolutely none.

JARVIS: Do you keep up your work at all? I mean your proper work.

HELEN: Reading Aeschylus doesn't pay the rent, I'm afraid.

DAMSINSKI: I received last week a great treasure. One whole bottle of the real Macoysky from a friend. And just because I refused to carry a table up to some savage's room, she picked up the bottle and threw it into the dustbin. Smish-smesh!

EDWARD: That seems to be getting a habit with her.

DAMSINSKI: It's the nigskys. They've made her a barbarian. It's infectious.

EDWARD: Oh, for God's sake! Stop using that word!

HELEN [*to* JARVIS]: Will you move into college? They can look after you there.

JARVIS [*coldly*]: I do not require looking after, thank you. I shall buy a small flat in the town.

HELEN: But you can't cook, for example.

JARVIS: What one person can do – moderately – another can copy.

EDWARD: You could help her in some ways, surely?

DAMSINSKI: Why? She has perfectly good fetchers and carriers without expecting a half-dead man of refinement to do the work of serfs! God made blacks for carrying. They can't think, so the Almighty gave them strong backs, instead. All His Creation serves a purpose.

[*He crosses himself and leaves.* EDWARD *stands quivering with clenched fists.*]

HELEN: What about the Peace League? I imagine that must keep you busy.

JARVIS: I do not derive satisfaction from that organization any more. It is becoming obvious, I should have thought, that world peace is to be attained only with the demise of this planet.

HELEN: You don't mean that? You don't mean that, Father?

JARVIS: It is the same with public as with private endeavour. Promise dies – or is squandered . . . A good life wasted. That's all I see. Enjoy what you can of it.

[*He leaves also.*]

HELEN [*calling after him*]: I *am* enjoying! . . . I'm happy!

[EDWARD *and she rejoin each other in the Kilburn room. The light changes. Both are upset.*]

EDWARD: Two fathers alike in indignity. Mine the worse. All his life unused. Drained away in burps and bigotry. [*Pause.*] And I'm the same in the end. Terminally futile.

HELEN: I never said that!

EDWARD: But you'd be absolutely right. Do it or die – that's the iron law.

HELEN: Then do it! Do it! Or we'll stay here for the rest of our lives!

EDWARD [*seriously*]: Yes, I know . . . Look, here and now, stone-cold sober, I promise you: I will write a complete play. One totally finished play . . . Actually, it's been in my head for weeks. It's ready to go.

HELEN: Are you serious?

EDWARD: I've promised.

HELEN: Swear it! [*A sudden inspiration.*] – On your desk!

EDWARD: All right . . . [*Moving quickly to the desk and slapping his hand on it.*] I swear – by Rasputin!

HELEN: No, no! Serious!

EDWARD [*warmly*]: Then by our love. I swear to give you, within one year of this hour, one vast and glinting play. I swear to keep my nose to the grindstone, my arse to the chair, my hand from ever tearing up or starting anything else until it's done! [*He raises his hand in a ritual gesture of swearing.*] May I die in torment if I break this oath!

> [HELEN *takes a large envelope from the desk and gives it to* PHILIP.]

HELEN: And that night he left *this* on my pillow. A message for me. I'd like you to read it.

PHILIP: What is this?

HELEN: Something no one else has ever seen.

> [*He extracts two pieces of paper covered in blue writing and unfolds them.*]

PHILIP [*excited*]: Is this his writing?

HELEN: Yes.

PHILIP: Oh, my God. I've never actually seen a sample! It's wild! I mean, it's so assertive. So vigorous!

HELEN: Just read it, please.

PHILIP: Yes, yes of course. [*Reading.*] Ancient Greece. The Temple of Athena. Enter Perseus, a proud Hero in search of Glory. [*To* HELEN.] Perseus? Did he write a Perseus play? I never heard of that.

HELEN: No.

PHILIP: But is is a play? It looks like one.

HELEN: It's just a scene. Not intended to be acted. Let's call it part of our private correspondence – his and mine. The sort of thing biographers need to see.

PHILIP: You mean he saw himself as Perseus?

HELEN: Yes.

PHILIP: And you as Athena?

HELEN: Read it.

PHILIP: Yes, yes, of course . . .

[*A warning rumble of music. The light begins to change as* PHILIP *starts reading. The screens draw back. The wall of lava parts in the middle – and a ramp is seen to extrude from it like a golden walkway lowered into the room. This provides a path connecting the imagined mythological world to the middle of Edward's desk. Mist fills the empty space at the top: out of this –to triumphant music – walks the figure of* PERSEUS *wearing costume appropriate to a legendary young Greek Hero and a mask displaying an expression of eager hopefulness. He advances down the ramp and on to the desk, where he kneels in supplication, staring straight ahead. His voice as he calls out is heard on tape: it belongs to* EDWARD.]

PHILIP [*reading as this happens*]: Ancient Greece. The Temple of Athena. Enter Perseus, a proud Hero in search of Glory. At this moment, like most would-be Heroes in Greek legend, he has made an exceedingly foolish vow which he cannot possibly fulfil. In this scene he begs the help of Athena, cleverest Goddess in the sky, given to extricating passionate men from impossible situations – provided she is properly begged. Which involves first calling out all her names in the right order.

PERSEUS [*calling out*]: Athena Hellenica! Athena Scholastica! Athena Supportiva! Inspirer of the Fearful! Sustainer of the Scared! Appear to me now! A fool implores you.

[*Music swells. The light grows richer. Behind, in her chariot, appears the* GODDESS ATHENA, *carrying her long spear and a huge shield of brass. The mask she wears beneath her helmet denotes immense serenity. She is accompanied by two female spirits bearing gifts: these they display as* ATHENA *names them. Her voice is also on tape: it belongs to* HELEN. EDWARD *stands by as the scene is played, watching* HELEN *closely.*]

ATHENA: I hear you, Perseus! Why are you scared?

PERSEUS: I have made a vow and cannot keep it. Now I must spend the rest of my days in shame.

ATHENA: What vow?

PERSEUS: To kill the Gorgon. The snake-haired Gorgon, Medusa.

ATHENA: That was rash.

PERSEUS: Beyond rash! Her gaze turns all who meet it into stone.

ATHENA: It does.

PERSEUS: She lives on the Island of Immobility, which cannot be found, by land or sea!

ATHENA: It cannot.

PERSEUS: Then I am lost! I might as well be stone already! A statue for birds to rest on for eternity!

ATHENA: And cover your handsome face with droppings? No, I am the Protector of Youth, Perseus. I forgive rashness. No Gorgon will ever turn you into stone. You will become a Hero and return in triumph.

PERSEUS [*joyfully*]: Oh, Goddess!

ATHENA: Receive now my gifts! First, the Shoes of Swiftness taken from the feet of Hermes! Wear these and be lost to earth!

[*The spirits – each carrying one – raise them.*]

PERSEUS: *Flying?* Of course! Not land or sea, but air! [*Greedily.*] May I wear them now?

ATHENA: Patience! Next, the Cap of Darkness! Woven from the skin of dogs in the kennels of Hades. Wear it and be lost to sight!

[*A spirit lifts up a mysterious dog-headed cap.*]

PERSEUS [*excited*]: *Invisible!* Oh, wonderful! [*Reaching for it.*] May I wear that at least?

ATHENA [*sharply*]: *Patience, I said!* . . . You have to be taught restraint, my friend.

PERSEUS: Forgive me!

ATHENA: Now, the Sickle of Adamant, with which Cronos, father of Zeus, wounded the sky. No other blade can cut the Gorgon's neck.

[*The other spirit raises this object.*]

[*Raising herself*]: Last, the Shield of Showing! My own shield, Perseus, never lent before! Look at the monster in *this* alone. The only way Man may ever see truth – by *reflection!* Take it and kill well. I allow you now the Sacred Gift of Vengeance!

[*She extends the brass shield.* PERSEUS *turns and takes it. We see his face reflected in its shining convex surface.*]

PERSEUS: Oh, Goddess, how may I thank you? What gift can a mortal make to you?

ATHENA: Only one. The Gorgon's head! The snake-crowned head itself. Set it there – in the centre of my shield, where it can never harm again. Swear to do this.

PERSEUS [*touching the shield*]: I swear!

ATHENA: 'May I die in torment if I break this oath.'

[PERSEUS *echoes* EDWARD'*s ritual gesture of a few minutes ago.*]

PERSEUS: May I die in torment if I break this oath!

ATHENA: Good. Now go.

[PERSEUS *walks triumphantly across the stage accompanied by the two spirits.* ATHENA *calls after him.*]

ATHENA: One last word! From the Gorgon's veins two bloods will flow. That from the left kills. That from the right cures. Understand.

PERSEUS [*pausing*]: What does it mean? [*Insistently.*] What does that mean, Goddess?

[*But* ATHENA *retires into the mist, and the drawbridge rises after her.* PERSEUS *leaves downstage with the attendant spirits. The music fades.*

PHILIP: You said this wasn't a play.

HELEN: It wasn't. I told you it was written for our eyes alone.

PHILIP: Did he communicate with you like that all the time, my father? Leaving messages on your pillow disguised as scenes?

HELEN: Not usually. I actually possess only two of them . . . Well, to be precise, three.

PHILIP: Well, this one is obviously very personal. The Gorgon – a monster who turned people to stone – that's his creative paralysis, surely. He needed your help to kill it. Is that what he meant?

HELEN [*nodding*]: Good.

PHILIP: By the way, is that true, what Athena said about the Gorgon's veins? Two bloods – one killing, one curing?

HELEN: Oh, yes. After her death the blood that cures was gathered up and given to Aesculapius. He became the patron saint of Medicine.

PHILIP: You obviously *are* very learned.

[EDWARD *kisses her brow.*]

EDWARD: That's who you are – Athena! Brave and learned Goddess! Bountiful, inspiring and wise! [*Abruptly.*] Now – the new play!

HELEN: Tell me about it.

EDWARD: What do you know of the Iconoclasts?

HELEN: Byzantium. Eighth century AD.

EDWARD: Good girl! Constantinople, the most amazing city in history. Its citizens actually fought to the death over religious images. Cataracts of blood were shed to worship or destroy them. And quite rightly.

HELEN: Why?

EDWARD: Because the quarrel enshrines the most fundamental division in the human race: between abstract mind and concrete mind. Between those who believe God is always invisible – and those who need *illustration* to make them perceive it ... This is the age-old fight which under Cromwell smashed almost every statue made in England over five hundred years. It turned *Islam* into a labyrinth of abstract patterns, and forced three quarters of the world's *Jews* to become secular in order to escape the aridness of the Second Commandment: Thou Shalt Make No Graven Image ... Iconoclasts say: God is complete. We can't make any part of Him. Their opponents say: No! He's not finished! He needs *us* to complete Him, and make Him apparent.

HELEN: And which side are you on?

EDWARD: The makers, of course. Anyone can break! Formed beauty is a vindication of Man ... I shall call the play *Icons*.

HELEN: Splendid!

EDWARD: Every word will be written in *red* – unflinching red! ... I'll never use blue again! Blue is the colour of defeat. And I'll do the whole thing on a new kind of paper. I shall literally turn over new leaves!

[*He scoops up all the smaller pages with blue ink on them and drops them into the waste-paper basket, then sits at the desk.*]

HELEN: He began to write at once – in a fever! The new paper was an absurd luxury. Hand-made rag from an art shop. Impossibly beyond our means.

EDWARD: Absolute necessity! You must be a God when you are creating a world. Do you think Jehovah chose any old shale when He wrote the Ten Commandments? You can bet it was the best stone in the Sinai desert.

[*She laughs. He starts quickly to cut them into lengths with a sharp wooden-handled mat-knife, first slipping a piece of cardboard beneath each one he cuts to protect the desk. We hear the sound, at first naturalistically, of the blade slicing through the paper.*]

HELEN: It came in sheets about three feet long. He'd have to trim it down to size with a special tool. What they call a mat-knife. It has a hollow wooden handle where you can store the blades. They – they are extremely sharp.

[*She stops, plainly distressed. The sound of the cutting blade becomes amplified. It grows louder, then louder. She seems to hear it, and turns abruptly away. The sound stops.* EDWARD *starts to write frantically in red on the first cut page, covering it furiously.* HELEN *stands rigid.*]

PHILIP: Helen? Are you OK. . . . Helen?

HELEN [*not looking at him, attempting to control herself*]: You'll find it on the desk. You may look at it there, if you wish. Be careful how you hold it.

[PHILIP *looks at her curiously, then reaches over the desk – where* EDWARD *continues to write urgently – and picks up the mat-knife.*]

PHILIP: My God, that's a wicked thing, isn't it? I see what you mean!

HELEN [*stiffly*]: I'd hear it cutting through the paper first thing in the day – before I went off to the travel agency. When I got back at night there'd always be a pile covered in red . . .

[*Pause. She is still upset.*]

PHILIP: Helen? . . . Is there anything wrong?

HELEN [*sharply*]: I'm telling you! Please listen! [*Recovering.*] I'm sorry, but this is really the stuff you should treasure. How the man worked. How we both did . . .

PHILIP [*abashed*]: Of course. I'm sorry.

[*He sits hastily at his notebook and works the pencil-sharpener.*]

HELEN: Every night when I got back he'd be ready. Sometimes with whole scenes. Sometimes just one, in ten versions. I would be audience, critic, actress, reading it aloud – giving it life outside his head.

[EDWARD *thrusts pages at her.*]

HELEN: The play simply welled up out of his deepest obsessions.

PHILIP: Beauty and violence.

HELEN: Yes.

PHILIP: I give a lecture on him called that.

HELEN: Yes, well, you wouldn't have seen the beauty if I hadn't dealt with the violence.

PHILIP: What do you mean?

HELEN [*handing him a page covered in the red writing*]: Read this. One of the many scenes you never saw onstage.

> [PHILIP *looks at it, as* EDWARD *watches her. Immediately the light changes and austere Byzantine chanting is heard. The shutters open, and the figure of the* EMPRESS IRENE *appears, encrusted in jewels. Two cloaked women attendants assist her on to the desk. Two guards lead in a captive young man and throw him down at her feet. As before, the faces of all these characters are masked and their voices are heard only on tape.*]

PHILIP [*reading*]: The scene becomes the Purple Room in the Palace of the Eastern Empire, fifteenth day of August 757 AD. Imperial guards cast down before the Empress Irene her son Constantine the Sixth, destroyer of religious images.

> [*As the* EMPRESS IRENE *mimes her fury,* EDWARD *excitedly declaims the scene to* HELEN.]

EDWARD: Empress Irene speaks: What mercy can be for him who seeks to blind God? You have scraped from His temple walls the eyes of Christ. Now your own eyes must pay . . . Constantine speaks: No!

PHILIP [*reading*]: The Gongs of Extinction sound. The guards carry in a burning brazier.

> [EMPRESS IRENE *claps her hands. One guard marches offstage. The other holds fast the young* EMPEROR'S *arms.*)

EDWARD: Constantine speaks: Oh, mother – No! No! No! . . . Empress Irene speaks: Live now without the world you have disdained!

PHILIP [*reading*]: They take from the fire the white-hot Spike of Retribution.

[*The guard returns bearing a sharp weapon of iron.*]

EDWARD: Constantine speaks: Mother, in the name of God! God's mother! His *mother!*

[*He raises it and applies it to an eye-socket of* CONSTAN-TINE's *mask. The* EMPEROR *screams and the whole scene freezes.*]

HELEN [*to* EDWARD]: No! . . . *No!*

[*Light changes back.* EDWARD *and* HELEN *confront each other in front of the frozen figures of Byzantium.*]

EDWARD: What's the matter?

HELEN: It's appalling.

EDWARD: It actually happened. She did it.

HELEN: I don't care. You still can't show it.

EDWARD: Why not?

HELEN: Because it's too much. Measure is everything. The Greeks knew that. They never showed violence onstage.

EDWARD: But Shakespeare did, and he's the final guide.

HELEN: Look, please. It'll be much more effective *off.* Write a *speech* for her instead, addressing the assembled people. Explaining to them exactly why she has done this unspeakable thing. It's so dreadful it has to be excused anyway.

EDWARD: Not to me. It was absolutely right what she did! That man was a murderer of beauty. There's no worse crime in the world.

HELEN: Oh, Edward, for Heaven's sake!

EDWARD: I'm serious. Constantine deserved his blinding as Agamemnon deserved his chopping. What fitter punishment could there be for a man who made war on pictures – to have all pictures taken away from him for ever?

PHILIP: Wow!

EDWARD: Smashers of art, like him or Cromwell, should be smashed up themselves. What you want is simply avoidance. Niminy-wiminy hiding!

PHILIP: All the same, you must have had your way.

[EDWARD *returns to his desk and writes.*]

HELEN: Yes, in the end. Thank goodness. He dismissed everyone from the stage but the Empress, and substituted the speech I'm sure you know.

[CONSTANTINE *and the soldiers leave the stage. The* EMPRESS IRENE *and her attendants remain.* EDWARD *sulkily thrusts another page at* HELEN.]

PHILIP: The defence of icons, to the crowd?

HELEN: Yes.

PHILIP [*quoting*]: I blinded my son because he blinded you! He prevented you from seeing God!

HELEN [*daring him*]: Can you go on?

PHILIP: Er . . . Ten thousand icons Constantine destroyed! Ten thousand images made by Christ for *you*!

[*The masked* EMPRESS IRENE *gestures elaborately, as* PHILIP *speaks with more confidence.*]

Twice He has appeared on earth! Once in flesh, now again in *paint*! Here in our city, holy men were lifted suddenly into ecstasy! Their hands were guided directly by His hands! Their brushes – dipped in the sweat of adoration – Let His unquenchable tenderness shine through the pigment!

HELEN: Well done!

PHILIP [*finishing with bravado, as the figure of the* EMPRESS IRENE *gestures with him*]: This is the amazing and the appalling truth. God's Son said, 'I will be seen again by Man!' And *my* son said, '*No! I forbid it!*'

HELEN [*joining in with him*]: What penalty is harsh enough for that?

[*The light goes down quickly on the* EMPRESS IRENE, *who leaves the stage assisted by helpers. The shutters close.*]

HELEN: It made a wonderful climax to the first act.

PHILIP: It still does.

HELEN: All the same, he resented me for making him write it. It was the start of his real resentment.

PHILIP: Resentment?

HELEN: Oh, yes. [*Approaching the desk where* EDWARD *sits writing furiously.*] Your father was a dark man, Philip. I don't know the word. Maybe there isn't one. Maybe you'll tell me what it is . . .

[*Pause. Wind.*]

That time, though, working together on the play, that was our best. Sometimes we'd stay up all night. I'd go back to my office next morning without any sleep at all. He, of course, would simply tumble into bed for the day.

PHILIP: Did you mind that?

HELEN: Of course not. [*She looks at him directly.*] Write this down. I lived by his need for me. Nothing else. That play was my child by him. My firstborn – and best. The only one truly balanced.

[PHILIP *writes.*]

EDWARD [*holding up more pages*]: Your *offspring*! Lovely word! . . . I promise you, there'll be many. And they will give you, I can tell you, far more pleasure than any children of flesh. We don't need those, Learned. Truly.

PHILIP: Did he ask you if *you* needed them?

HELEN: Never.

PHILIP: And that was his attitude always? All the time?

HELEN: Absolutely. [*Pause.*] You see, there had been one, right at the beginning.

PHILIP [*startled*]: I'm sorry? You mean a child?

HELEN: I became pregnant while we were in Greece. When we got back he found me a clinic in a London suburb. A dingy, hidden place. The baby was – dispensed with. He made it a condition.

PHILIP: Of marrying you?

HELEN: I agreed. I had to.

[*She moves around her husband, who is writing faster than ever over the big sheets of paper.*]

PHILIP: Why?

HELEN: It would have ended us otherwise. We had no

money. We had to borrow, as it was, from one of his old girlfriends for the operation. They weren't cheap . . . We lived in just that one room in Kilburn – no hiding from the crying and the mess. He'd have left me. He more or less told me so.

EDWARD: I can't be doing with all that, Learned. Babies are impossible for me . . . It's a matter of choice, actually.

PHILIP: And you chose him?

HELEN: Of course! What I had with him was irreplaceable. And *there* [*She points to the growing pile of manuscript.*] – *that* was *our* parenting! Our unique child . . . I watched it being born, limb by limb. The only kind he would ever love.

[*She looks radiantly at* EDWARD *working.*]

PHILIP [*quietly*]: Tell me, what was it? Boy or girl?

HELEN: A boy.

[*Pause.*]

PHILIP [*tightly*]: And he still never mentioned me to you, his . . . other one? Even during all that?

HELEN: Never.

PHILIP: So when, then? Please, can't you tell me now? It's really that important to me. When did you discover about me?

HELEN: In order, Philip. You'll know soon enough . . . Let's give him his triumph first.

[*She walks around the desk as she speaks.*]

He wrote the second half of the play in one continuous burst. No hang-ups at all. The rituals and litanies of Byzantium conjured up with such boldness. Even the races in the Hippodrome. On the first night, when we finally got it produced – and that took for ever – the audience simply stood up in a body. It wasn't all that usual in England then.

[*Applause. Members of the audience come in quickly, applauding.* EDWARD *stands proudly, smiling and shaking hands.*]

PHILIP: It made his name overnight.

[DAMSINSKI *suddenly enters, wearing evening dress.*]

DAMSINSKI: Bravo! Bravo! An absolute smesh, my boy! A smish-smesh hit! I salute you profoundly.

[*He falls on his knees before* EDWARD.]

EDWARD: Oh, for Christ's sake!

DAMSINSKI [*declaiming*]: No! This is the homage of one proud old dada to his brilliant boy!

[*He kisses* EDWARD'*s shoe.*]

HELEN: He did that right in front of everyone, in the foyer of the theatre.

DAMSINSKI [*to the amused crowd*]: A salute, absolutely, to my formidable son! Look at him! A chip off the old blocksky! [*He rises and embraces* EDWARD.] I am sorry, but your mother was a little too busy to come.

EDWARD: I understand.

DAMSINSKI: But I will tell her she has made a giant! We together – her and me – giantmakers!

[*He leaves in triumph. The crowd disperses.* JARVIS *comes in.*]

HELEN: My father saw the play too, later, at a matinée. He'd declined, of course, to attend the first night. [*To him.*] You could have asked me for a ticket.

JARVIS: It was a whim. I was passing the theatre.

HELEN: And did you care for it at all?

JARVIS: I found it flashy. The modern theatre, in my view, only pretends to deal with profundities. Clever pictorialism is no substitute for serious insight.

HELEN: We are moving, you know.

JARVIS: To a better neighbourhood?

HELEN: Will you come and see us, please?

JARVIS: I do not care for London, as you know. I do well enough here.

[*He leaves the stage. A telephone rings loudly.* EDWARD, *seated downstage, picks it up out of the basket of books.*]

EDWARD: Hallo? . . . [*Excited.*] Oh, *hallo!* I'm a great admirer . . . Well, that's very generous of you. [*He hangs up. To*

HELEN.] That was James Fuller, the Byzantine scholar. He says I've got it essentially right.

HELEN [*happy*]: Hurrah!

[*The phone rings again instantly.*]

EDWARD: Hallo! [*Excited.*] Well, thank you! Come to dinner Thursday night! [*To* HELEN, *replacing the phone.*] James Fogg, the poet.

HELEN [*to* PHILIP]: We had to hire a smart Knightsbridge firm to cook for us practically every evening.

[*A debutante-like young woman enters, beating an egg in a copper bowl with a balloon whisk. The phone rings again.*]

EDWARD: Hallo! No, I'm sorry, I really can't. I just *can't*! I haven't a single evening free for two weeks!

HELEN: And, of course, a secretary, to deal with all the letters. And, naturally, a full-time maid.

[*A maid enters, running a vacuum cleaner, and from the other side a secretary carrying a bundle of letters and a notebook.*]

EDWARD [*taking a letter from the pile*]: This one's from the director Alan Rusk. He calls *Icons* the best new play in twenty years.

HELEN: Really?

EDWARD: You sound surprised.

HELEN: Well, they're pretty strong words, don't you think?

EDWARD: No. I'd call them fair comment, actually.

[*Pause. Light change. All freeze.* HELEN *stares at her husband, but speaks to* PHILIP.]

HELEN: Almost immediately it went.

PHILIP: What?

HELEN: The health in the situation. Overnight it seemed . . .

PHILIP: How do you mean?

HELEN: It was as if an intense light had been switched on – one of those they use to make plants grow quickly. Only what was growing in him was alarming. The wrong side of confidence.

[*The three girls go off quickly.*]

EDWARD [*taking a letter from his secretary's hand as she goes*]: Do you know the American director, Alan Glazer? He calls me an instant classic . . . Well, why not?

[*He goes on reading.*]

HELEN: Of course the theatre world didn't help matters. All that inflated feeling around him every day. Constant praise. Constant flattery. And all the *in*constant rest of it.

[*Soft popular music.*]

HELEN: The usual inconstancy – casual – secretive – and the far from secret vanity growing with it.

[*The three women reappear transformed – by quick removal of wigs, cook's apron, maid's overall and secretary's coat – into three sexy and attractively dressed young girls. They stand at the corners of the stage, swaying to the music.*]

It was inevitable, I suppose. After all, I was the wife. Privation, rewrites and rationed drinks. Life suddenly held better pleasures.

[EDWARD *picks up the phone, mouthing secretively into it and leaning forward meaningfully towards each girl in turn.*]

HELEN: It's amazing what people accept, when they are needed. I showed nothing. [*Ironically.*] I was his muse, remember: above jealousy. The Noble Presence, without which the work could not be achieved . . . I took the role. And stuck to it – till it stuck to me.

[*The girls leave the stage.* EDWARD *rises and moves to his desk.*]

Six years of that. Six years by my own choice . . . Well beyond the birth of our second child.

PHILIP: You mean the Cromwell play?

HELEN: Yes. *Prerogative.* We worked on that together, as before. But it was much harder now to get him to listen. Choosing Cromwell's England as his next subject seemed to make his writing more violent than ever. First, quite legitimately, he wrote a scene showing the smashing of countless masterpieces of English art.

EDWARD [*holding up one of his large pieces of paper covered in red writing*]: The nave of an Anglican church: high-baroque sanctuary! Shafts of ruby and topaz falling on noble catafalques. Golden Christs, and marble Madonnas, smiling on the world. Suddenly the whole glorious space is invaded by Puritan thugs in metal – led by the General himself, Oliver the Grim!

[*We see the reflection of a glorious stained-glass window – a primitive crucifixion on a blazing red background – clearly thrown on to the white floor. At the same moment an iron-masked* CROMWELL, *in breastplate and armour, marches in and mounts the desk. He carries a massive sword. Downstage two soldiers, similarly masked, wheel on a life-size medieval Christ beautifully fashioned in wood.*]

CROMWELL [*taped voice: stern and relentless*]: Strike! Strike from these windows every piece of gaudy glass interposed between you and God's clear firmament! These only are the needs of Man – the shining sky above him, and his shining soul within!

[*The soldiers turn and strike upwards with their swords. A tremendous crash of glass. The reflection of the window disappears, to be replaced by one of an empty, ruined frame as white light floods the stage.*]

Now smash in the name of God this English nursery! Break, I tell you, all these dolls – these painted Christs and Virgins! Are we infants, to have need for dolls? Leave only wood – plain as humility! Stone hard as his sepulchre! Do as I bid – and free yourselves from *dollatry*!

[*One of the soldiers strikes off the head of Christ, the other dribbles it like a football and finally kicks it into the wings.* CROMWELL *marches out the way he came; the soldiers leave downstage pulling the decapitated Christ after them. The light changes back.*]

HELEN [*to* PHILIP]: Understand – I did not object to that, shocking as it was. It was terrible and legitimate. But then the climax suddenly went too far. Extreme Edward at his most extreme.

EDWARD [*snatching up a piece of paper covered in red writing*]: This bully permitted all that destruction in the name of his hateful God of Hosts. He created the most pitiless army England ever saw to serve Him: iron regiments for an iron God. He even shut all theatres and silenced all plays . . . I want my audience to *rejoice* in the man's death! And this is how to do it. [*He thrusts the paper at her.*] Use his head.

HELEN: What do you mean?

EDWARD: Not Christ's. *His own! – Cromwell's!* Did you know after he was buried they dug him up again? Hacked off the head and stuck it on a pole. It rotted there for six months outside Westminster Hall.

HELEN: And you want to show *that*?

EDWARD: Read.

> [HELEN *reads. Instantly the two soldiers come on again, one with the rotting head of* CROMWELL *which he jams on a long pole held by the other. Then they elevate it, centre stage, away from the audience – and freeze.*]

HELEN [*reading*]: The head of Cromwell is paraded through the crowd. This object – once reverenced by some almost as passionately as Christ's head itself – is now treated like one of the countless effigies his followers smashed. This symbol of murderous Puritanism is now destroyed before our eyes by a crowd of English men and women whose spirit it destroyed when living. At the final curtain they tear the head in pieces and throw them exultantly to the applauding audience.

PHILIP: Jesus!

HELEN [*to* EDWARD]: I don't believe this. I don't believe this, Edward!

EDWARD: It'll be tremendous!

HELEN: It'll be childish.

EDWARD: What?

HELEN: Completely childish.

EDWARD: Yes – and profound. Both. The wonder of theatre!
... It'll obviously be a prop, that head – canvas and paper
– but by the miracle of art it will become transubstantiated!
The object will be simultaneously canvas and flesh. The
scene will be simultaneously infantile and deep: a group of
actors shouting, and a communal Execration. The kind of
iconoclasm which can actually liberate people – like tearing
down statues of dictators in public squares.

> [*He goes to the desk and takes out of it a bottle of red wine
> and a glass.*]

HELEN [*hotly*]: And either way it will be awful! ... If they
don't buy it, it'll just be silly. If they do, it will be worse:
degrading. As degrading as the original act of digging him
up! ... You are dealing with a great man, for Heaven's
sake! Cromwell was one of the greatest Englishmen who
ever lived. Someone actually inspired by real principle for
a change, probably the purest ever found in this country.

EDWARD: Really? Well, you tell that to the Irish he slaugh-
tered in thousands. Tell it to their descendants who are
now slaughtering *us* because of what he did. The terrorists!
... We're dealing with three centuries of ache for that
revenge! Three hundred and fifty years for it to become
diseased.

HELEN: All revenge is diseased.

EDWARD: No – only when it's kept unfulfilled. Then it festers.
Then it ranges through modern streets looking for *anyone* to
answer it. It murders babies in department stores. Soldier-
boys tootling trumpets on bandstands. Old women tottering
about railway stations! That's centuries of denied blood –
ravening! ... And the only thing we can do to prevent it
infecting *us*, the English, and turning us into monsters all
over again, is to revenge ourselves *now*, while our feeling is
just! Kill every terrorist we capture, instantly, in proper rage!
Proper, proper rage! That way we can stay clean.

[*Pause.* EDWARD *pours himself a glass of wine.*]

HELEN: I find that absolutely appalling.

EDWARD: It is the playwright's duty to appal. Tear an audience out of moral catalepsy.

HELEN [*growing more and more upset*]: It is a playwright's duty, Edward, to be *fair*. To his subject, and its complexity . . . Cromwell was a complex, ardent man. You can't just reduce him to a simple effigy of evil . . . [*Simply, with great appeal.*] If you don't want to listen to me, then at least hear *him*: Cromwell himself. It was one of my father's favourite quotations: 'I beseech you in the bowels of Christ, think it possible you may be mistaken.' That's what the man said. [*Earnestly.*] Please. [*Pause.*] Please.

[*Silence.* EDWARD *sits at the desk. Then deliberately he picks up a pile of papers covered in the red writing and tears them across. The soldiers and their pole immediately leave the stage with the head impaled.*]

[*To* PHILIP.] He put into Cromwell's mouth instead, to end the play, a wonderful speech of defeated idealism. Everyone loved it.

PHILIP: I know. I read it sometimes to my classes. It's one of his finest things.

HELEN: Everyone but he himself.

EDWARD: Avoidance, that's all. *Again.* Endless bloody avoidance.

HELEN [*to* EDWARD]: Under everything, you know I'm right.

[*Pause.*]

EDWARD: How long do you want me to keep pleasing your father, Learned?

HELEN [*to* EDWARD]: What do you mean?

EDWARD: Parvus-Jarvis: right there inside you!

HELEN: I hope he is. I hope so, Edward. [*To* PHILIP.] He had died, poor man, just before the play opened. Alone in his little flat, of a sudden heart attack. Never having spoken one single good word to my husband. Or about him . . . I went alone to the funeral.

[JARVIS *enters and diagonally crosses the stage. She watches him go.*]

[*Bitterly.*] He should have waited just a little longer. He'd have had his revenge. Indeed he would.

[*Light change.* EDWARD *takes off his coat to reveal a white short-sleeved T-shirt. He pours more red wine into his glass and drinks.*]

HELEN: I remember the exact day when it all stopped in Edward for good – any sense of measure. When I knew absolutely I would never again be able to influence his work, or contain it. November the eighth, 1987.

[*Radio announcements.* EDWARD *and* HELEN *listen.*]

BBC MALE ANNOUNCER: This morning a bomb exploded at a War Memorial in the town of Enniskillen, Northern Ireland. It happened without warning as a crowd was assembling for a Remembrance Day Service, commemorating the dead of two world wars. At least eight people have been killed and many more injured.

IRISH FEMALE ANNOUNCER: Among the dead is Marie Wilson, a twenty-year-old nurse. Her father has said that he forgives the terrorists responsible. 'I bear them no ill will,' he said. 'I bear them no grudge.'

EDWARD: *Incredible!* What a terrible thing to say!

HELEN: I think it's glorious! It's possibly the most moving thing I ever heard.

EDWARD: Of course. You would! You and your friends.

HELEN: What friends? I have no friends apart from yours.

EDWARD: The Niminys, of course. The Brigade of Avoiders!

HELEN: Oh, please!

EDWARD: Don't you ever get tired of being fair, Helen? Of 'understanding' the other side?

HELEN: Please just stop it, will you?

EDWARD: I find it completely beyond belief! Our bleating parliament can watch something like this, and not legislate death at once for those who did it. *That* is actually true evil! Can't you see it has become a vice, your fairness? How it's castrating us?

[*Pause. He looks at her earnestly.*]

There is a deep thirst in this world for right. Don't you ever feel that? I want to speak for people all over the world who spend their days choking back *fury* at the tolerated beasts on this planet, because it's not mature to feel unappeasable rage – unappeasable *lust* for justice! It's *our job* here to make justice – not God's. Because without it we have no meaning.

[*He rises, taking the open bottle of red wine.*]

I am going to write a new play. I see it with absolute clarity: clear and clean. An I.R.A. bomb explosion in the toy department of a large London store. Mothers and children blown to pieces: dolls and teddy bears spattered with blood and brains. Among the victims, the little daughter of a lady Member of Parliament – hitherto passionately against the death penalty. The killers escape to Ireland. The M.P. knows they will never be punished. So she becomes herself the instrument of their rebuke. She resigns her job and dedicates her life to tracking down the ringleader in Belfast, luring him to a hired room, and making him her captive.

HELEN [*tight*]: Yes? And?

EDWARD: She achieves justice. For the man and herself.

HELEN: How?

EDWARD: Executing him – ritually – before the eyes of the audience. Not sadistically, but in the sanative way of gaining peace. The hallowed, health-giving peace of Clytemnestra, slaughtering her husband in that bath. Setting at rest the spirit of her screaming daughter . . . As the killer finally expires in that sordid little room, that woman – a

mild, decent, humanitarian woman – will dance before
him, in release.

[*Pause*.]

HELEN [*hard*]: I see. Well, that should *expire* your career.

EDWARD: What do you mean?

HELEN: The audience will simply reject you.

EDWARD: They'd never do that to me. I have my audience –
and they trust my voice.

HELEN: Well, try it then, and see! Everything you've built
will be in ruins. Everything *we* have built.

EDWARD [*coolly*]: Ah, that's your trouble in the end, isn't it,
Learned? Deep down you're afraid of being unapproved
. . . Well, that's the final ordeal a writer has to endure . . .
If you had wanted perpetual respectability, you should
have stayed in the house of your safe liberal daddy.

HELEN: That's not fair, and you know it!

EDWARD [*fiercely*]: Look, for God's sake, terrorism is the
single most dreadful new thing in our world. Any playwright worth his salt has to face that.

HELEN [*exploding back*]: All right, then face it! You still don't
have to debase *me* at the same time!

EDWARD [*in fury*]: You! Always *you*!

HELEN: Everyone in the theatre! Every single person watching! [*She stares at him, her words suddenly tumbling out of her.*]
Surely, surely we've learnt one thing over the ages? The
dead have to be *resisted*! When they call for blood, we have
to be deaf! . . . We have to be *bigger* than they were, or
what's the point?

[*Pause*.]

You go on about passion, Edward. But have you never
realized there are many, many kinds? – Including a passion
to kill our own passion when it's wrong. I'm not just being
clever. The truest, hardest, most adult passion isn't stamping
and geeing ourselves up. It's refusing to be led by rage
when we most want to be. That means every time a bomb

goes off, yes, and every time a baby is killed, and every other filthy thing that makes you sick with fury. Stubbornly continuing to say No to blood. All right, the Greeks wouldn't have understood this, but they were savages, finally. The whole of their country *ran* with blood. It was all entrails and screaming: no pity for anyone. They had Gods to take the big view *for* them. Athena could come down suddenly and stop the boys fighting, like a schoolmistress in a playground. We haven't got *anyone* to do that. We're the boys and the mistress, *both* – that's the impossible and wonderful thing about *us*! No other being in the universe can change itself by conscious will: it is *our privilege alone*. To take out inch by inch this spear in our sides that goads us on and on to bloodshed – and still make sure it doesn't take our guts with it. My dad invented that image. My liberal old daddy. He was the only person I ever met who showed me a point to life . . . There's meaning if you want meaning!

[*Pause.*]

EDWARD [*admiringly*]: Bravo! That was terrific. Jarvis-Parvus must have done something right to make you shine like that. God knows how, but I honour him for it. I really do . . . It was all twaddle – every word – but it made you glint. And that's all that counts in the end. Come here to me . . .

HELEN: Don't be condescending, please.

EDWARD: I mean it! I mean it, Learned!

HELEN [*suddenly angry and near tears*]: Well, *I* mean *this*, Edward – and I mean it absolutely. Any play, for whatever reason, which says: 'Take the way of blood and then dance afterwards' is *evil*! . . . Just that.

[*Pause. They glare at each other.*]

EDWARD [*calmly*]: At the end of my play, the actress will show an ordinary lady, sane but transfigured. She will stand and look out at the people sitting in their rows. Her hands will be wet with the blood of the man who blew her little daughter into pieces. And gently, with the gentleness of the truly justified, she will say to them: '*You*. Not your neighbour: you! Do not live forever in contempt of life. Judge. It is your right. Don't be afraid. Only acceptance can destroy you – perpetual acceptance of obscenity. Take from these murderers the life they have violated – and feel it returning into *you*.' Then she will go out into the theatre and pass among them with outstretched arms, holding a cloth. They will feel between her fingers the fluid which for them will now be blood, and they will wipe it from her, to signify that for them she did right. Then they may kiss her hands. And the theatre will reclaim its moral power.

[*He turns to her.*]

[*Gravely.*] I will tell you only one truth, my girl. Understand it. There are people who become literally unforgivable. There are such things as unforgivable acts – beyond the pale of pardon.

HELEN [*as gravely in return*]: I do not believe that. And I never will.

EDWARD: You have to. [*Pause.*] I must make you. Or you will never finally know life.

[*Suddenly he pours the whole bottle of red wine over his head. It stains his white T-shirt and falls in a great scarlet splash on to the white floor. He stretches out his hands to her, dripping wine. She screams with horror and turns away from him. There is an immediate light change.* EDWARD *leaves.* HELEN *stands distressed.*]

PHILIP: What is it? . . . What is it, Helen?

HELEN [*wildly, to* PHILIP]: Why did you come? . . . Why did you have to?

PHILIP: I don't understand.

HELEN: Why didn't you just keep away, when I told you? We're stopping now. This minute! . . . No more!

PHILIP: We can't do that!

HELEN: Just go! . . . Now! . . . Please, at once!

PHILIP: We made a bargain!

HELEN: Just go, Philip. No more talk! Leave here now. Now!

PHILIP [*going to her in sudden fury*]: No! . . . No more of *this*! Stop-start-stop! . . . [*He grabs her arms.*] I'm not leaving, do you understand me? You're going *on* now, to the end. No more of this *nonsense*! *Damn it!* No more!

   [*In his anger he grips her too hard. She cries out. He releases her. Pause.* HELEN *feels her bruised arm.* PHILIP *moves away, ashamed.*]

Jesus! Oh, Jesus! [*Pause.*] But I'm not a child . . . Stop all this protection! The man ignored me all his life. I can take anything from him, dead . . . Look at me: I'm not afraid.

   [*Pause.* HELEN *looks at him.*]

HELEN [*in an altered, hard voice*]: Very well. He did not stumble on that cliff, as they announced.

PHILIP [*startled*]: What?

HELEN: He did not stumble to his death, your father.

   [*Pause.*]

It's late now. Come back in the morning. I'll finish it for you.

PHILIP: What do you mean? . . . It was an accident, surely? *An accident!*

   [*Pause.*]

Helen? [*Crying out to her.*] Helen!

HELEN [*quietly*]: He will be real to you, Philip. He'll be real now — very soon.

   [*The wind blows. The light fades. The wine lies like a bright stain of blood between them.*]

END OF ACT TWO

ACT THREE

The next morning.

[*Sunlight pours through the closed shutters.* PHILIP *stands drinking coffee. His suitcase by the door.* HELEN *stands looking at him. The wind still blows lightly.*]

HELEN: You'll be off in an hour.

PHILIP: How weird. America seems so far away. Almost non-existent.

HELEN: Did you know that Freud called it a mistake?

PHILIP: America?

HELEN: I think it is, in your case. You're obviously European . . . Rather a pale one at the moment.

PHILIP: Is that surprising? I had little sleep.

HELEN: And less tonight.

[*He looks at her, startled.* KATINA *enters.*]

KATINA: *O kyrios theli gaithuraki?* (Does the gentleman wish a donkey?)

HELEN: She wishes to know if you want a donkey to take you down to the harbour?

PHILIP: Good God, no. Never again. [*To* KATINA, *miming.*] I'll walk, thank you.

[*He smiles at her. She glares back at him.*]

KATINA: *Tha sas po otan ftasi to karavi.* (I'll tell you when the boat appears.)

HELEN: She will tell you when the boat comes round the headland. That'll give you time. [*To* KATINA.] *Afisemas tora se parakalo.* (Leave us now, please.)

[*The housekeeper departs, scowling as usual.*]

PHILIP: She's glad I'm going.

HELEN: Oh, yes. What she'd really like is for me to go too. Then she could be the curator here and show the house to tourists. The face is made for pious recall, don't you think?

PHILIP: Please. I really feel half-crazy. What did you mean, last night? Not an accident.

[*Pause.*]

HELEN: Reach into the desk and take the next envelope you find there.

[PHILIP *extracts another large envelope from the drawer.*]

HELEN: The same evening when he spilt the wine, he left that for me to find on my bed. Like the other time.

PHILIP: Another Perseus scene?

HELEN [*bitterly*]: Yes. Only with a somewhat different Athena. This is how he saw me now. Read.

[PHILIP *takes out the page and reads it. Light change. Music. The cliff of lava parts again – the golden ramp is again lowered and* PERSEUS *appears on it, masked as before. On his feet are the winged Shoes of Swiftness, on his head is the Cap of Darkness, on his arm is Athena's great brass Shield of Showing. As before, his voice and that of the* GODDESS – EDWARD's *and* HELEN's – *are heard on tape.*]

PHILIP [*reading*]: Enter Perseus, armed and flying, geared for his task of rightful slaughter. He has flown far over forbidding oceans to the dreadful Island of Immobility. Silent bareness, littered with victims of the Gorgon's eyes. Stone farmers herding stone sheep; stone girls and babies . . . Hanging in the air the Hero sees suddenly below him the horror he has to face: the Gorgon, scaled and snouted – eyes fuming for new prey! She turns them upward: just in time, he looks into the Shield of Showing!

[*Hissing.* PERSEUS *illustrates what* PHILIP *reads.*]

He hovers trembling, prepared to strike. But *immediately* the clouds part and above him appears the Goddess he has worshipped blindly: Athena! Hitherto his helper!

ATHENA: I see you, Perseus! You are never invisible to me!
. . . Look down now at the Gorgon. *Directly at her!*

PERSEUS [*startled*]: Directly?

ATHENA: Not in the shield. Straight into her eyes!

PERSEUS: But you warned me not!

ATHENA [*warmly*]: Trust me! This now is the real purpose of
your journey. Not to kill, but to gain understanding. Look
down now unflinchingly at her you call monster. See how
each scale fits into flanks of breathing copper. Could you
make those? Look at her head of living snakes – the glitter
from enamelled skins. Could you make *those*? Try to see
now with eyes like mine, Perseus. Then if you still can do
it – kill what you can't create. Destroy a piece of God!
[*Intimately.*] Go on now – look directly, as I bid you.

PERSEUS [*trembling, staring still at the shield*]: I can't . . . I'm
afraid.

ATHENA: Look, I tell you. Simply turn your head!

PERSEUS: I can't! I must kill her! . . . I know!

ATHENA: Understand! All life is sacred. Take none! That is
my word.

PERSEUS: Then why give me weapons? The shield and the
sickle? Shoes to speed me?

ATHENA: Do not question Gods. Obey them!

PERSEUS [*violently*]: *No! No more!* I know what you want.
To kill me! See me turned to stone! . . . *Deceiver!* Deceiving,
lying, enfeebling Goddess! You seek to kill me by paralysis!
[*Dark music. Fearfully he turns, moves back to her, and takes
off her mask – to reveal another mask underneath, smiling
horribly. The theatre is filled with the terrible snarl of her
outrage.*]

ATHENA: Waaaaaaa!

PERSEUS: There! . . . There! . . . I see it! . . . Two spirits in
you – like the bloods in the Gorgon. Cure and kill! . . .
Athena the Goddess does not smile like that. That is
Athena – *woman*! Athena – jealous woman! Jealous of *me*!

ATHENA: Waaaaaaa!

PERSEUS: No more! . . . Never! . . . Henceforth I am *Perseus Unaided*! You are no longer my mentor or my guide!

ATHENA: Waaaaaaa!

[*The dark music grows.* PERSEUS *leaps off the desk and marches downstage.*]

PERSEUS: Now I kill the evil you permit on earth!

[ATHENA *retires defeated and the cliff face closes. The darkness grows. The Hero raises his sickle and staring into the shield, slashes violently downwards into the basket. A great scream is heard. When he lifts the weapon again, the head of the Gorgon is seen to be impaled on the end of the blade.* PERSEUS *lifts it into the shaft of light, the snakes wriggling upon it – and to triumphant music marches offstage. The light changes.*]

PHILIP [*handing* HELEN *back the page*]: My God!

HELEN: From that moment he never confided in me again. I was over.

[EDWARD *comes on and sits at the desk to write in a frenzy with fierce strokes of the pen, muttering and gesticulating to himself.*]

HELEN: He wrote the Irish play without a pause – hacking away, completely unreachable. I sound mad, I know, but our whole house seemed filled up with blackness. Worse, it came to fill the *theatre*.

[EDWARD *rises and stands rigidly by the desk beside his wife. They both watch.*]

At the first performance, as soon as the play began, the whole audience felt it coming off the stage. Some actually sat with their heads down.

[*A dark music begins. The shutters open and an Irish terrorist stumbles through them wearing sweater and trousers and a brutish white mask. A square gag is pasted across its painted mouth.* EDWARD *has placed a chair on the desk: the terrorist clumsily mounts and sits on it, his hands tied behind him. At*

*the same time the English mother of a murdered child described
earlier by* EDWARD *comes in. Her mask depicts a woman in
early middle age, her clothes are contemporary, and she carries
in her hand a knife. In stylized gesture she raises the weapon
high and ritually stabs the man three times. He dies.*]

HELEN: Then came the climax. When the Englishwoman
celebrated her release from the rage which had imprisoned
her since her little daughter's murder in the toy-shop –
when she stamped out her Dance of Holy Satisfaction – the
scene became very different from what Edward intended.

[*The woman raises her arms and begins to dance, at first in
slow motion.*]

It was not cleansing or cathartic, or any of the restorative
things he wanted Theatre to be.

[*The music comes up and grows wilder. The woman dances
around the desk. We hear laughter growing too, on tape,
derisive mirth filling the theatre, together with whistles, jeers,
mocking noises of encouragement and cries of 'Go it, girl!' etc.*
EDWARD *looks wildly around as the noise assails him from
all sides. Suddenly the woman freezes and the music stops.*]

HELEN: Of course he might still have put the laughter down
to bad choreography or the way she danced – but what
followed was undeniable, even to him. In the next five
minutes his mental world disintegrated before his eyes.

[*The woman moves slowly towards the audience holding out a
cloth with extended hands.*]

At the end, when the woman went into the audience to
have her hands wiped of blood by them – they turned
against her. Some still laughed. One said, 'Why don't you
just go to your dressing-room? You know where it is!'
Then, as she persisted, they got impatient.

[*The woman offers the cloth again and again.*]

Some started to boo. One of them shoved her. Another –
really angry – spat in her face. Edward sat beside me stock
still, as if he were being executed.

PHILIP: The reception was dreadful, I know.

[*Reviews of 'I.R.E.' are heard on tape.* EDWARD *stands listening, expressionless.*]

MALE: Appalling!

FEMALE: A middle-class woman abandoning everything civilization can teach her, slowly killing a trussed-up human being.

MALE: Then doing a sort of jig.

FEMALE: A kind of tribal knees-up we are expected to find 'liberating'.

MALE: With this play, the author tells us, the theatre is supposed to reclaim its moral power. All I saw it reclaim was hysteria.

MALE: In *I.R.E.* Damson misuses the power a playwright can briefly exert over his audience. At the end we get to see clearly just how nasty and exploitive his ideal of ultimate theatre really is. It is actually an attempt to seduce it into abetting mental and physical torture.

MALE: In a man of his abilities one can only deplore such deliberate perversion of the Drama.

FEMALE: The lamentable truth is clear: with this play Damson has simply ceased to be an artist.

[*Enter* DAMSINSKI.]

DAMSINSKI: I must admit I am displeased, my boy. A play is either art or it is nothing. This is Boola-Boola stuff . . . You sent me vodka as usual to drink the health of your new child. I have to tell you I cannot.

EDWARD: Then go dry.

DAMSINSKI: I will. Your mother will rejoice when I refuse to drink. Forgive me: I cannot salute. I go back to Cambridge now.

[*He leaves. Violently* EDWARD *unscrews a bottle of Russian vodka. Takes up a glass and fills it.*]

HELEN: And Edward drank *for* him ever after.

[*He sits and drinks, staring straight ahead.*]

All the acclaim of the past only weakened him now. He was like some huge tree whose roots have softened, so it falls in the first high wind. No struggle at all . . . It was more horrible than if he'd yelled.

PHILIP: The play only ran three nights, didn't it?

HELEN: We fled England the day it closed. And that's the proper word – 'fled'. He'd said he wanted to be unapproved. He got his wish.

PHILIP: And you had predicted it.

HELEN: Exactly.

PHILIP: Excuse me, but did you never think . . .?

HELEN: What?

PHILIP: Of not going with him?

HELEN: No. Not seriously.

PHILIP: You still felt . . . loyalty to what he'd been? What he might be again?

HELEN: Of course. Certainly I no longer felt it for myself. What *I* might have been. I had let it go too long.

PHILIP: It can't have been easy here.

HELEN: Oh, no. The silence between us had come to stay.

[EDWARD *drinks.*]

And the darkness. Like some unstoppable cancer in him. Five years growing in this room.

[*Wind softly.*]

PHILIP: He wrote nothing all that time?

HELEN: I kept thinking at least that might pass. That he'd suddenly start cutting that paper again. But he just sat there day after day – going away. Further and further. [*Pause.*] I know that what happened here finally was formed in that dark, long before he did it.

[EDWARD *laughs to himself, and drinks again.*]

Meanwhile, he had smaller revenges to inflict on me.

[*Lights up on two girl tourists with back-packs, standing on the terrace.*]

There are a great many tourists who come to this island.

Young girls on their own. He called them Back-Packlettes. He'd spend a long time in the bar – then bring one back deliberately to this house.

[EDWARD *rises to greet the first* – ELSE – *who comes into the living-room. Cool and smiling. She shakes* HELEN's *hand.*]

EDWARD: This is Else. She comes from Hanover.

HELEN: Ah.

ELSE [*German accent*]: I am most pleased to meet you, *ja*.

[HELEN *shakes her hand.*]

EDWARD: Her boyfriend is an actor. He spends the cold German nights reading plays to her aloud.

ELSE: *Ja,* aloud.

EDWARD: In bed. Most of Else's theatre has apparently been learnt in bed.

ELSE [*playfully*]: Sssh! [*To* HELEN.] He's vicked! Really!

HELEN: The young are so cool. They'd shake hands with me, then spend the evening drinking with my husband – chattering about their ambitions. After I'd gone to my room, they'd go to his. In the morning he'd lecture me about our need to be modern.

PHILIP: Didn't you protest? Surely you did?

HELEN [*exploding*]: I was scared, Philip. Afraid to leave. All I'd ever known was his world or my father's. I didn't want to bring it to an issue . . . Weak, wasn't it? Feeble to *your* modern eyes, no doubt.

PHILIP [*gently*]: I'm sorry.

[*The second girl* – MARY – *advances into the living-room from the terrace: she is wearing headphones.*]

EDWARD: And this is Mary. From sunny Australia. I suppose what we might fairly term an Outback-Packlette.

MARY: Pleased to meet you.

[HELEN *shakes her hand. Smiling.*]

EDWARD: Mary has an advanced taste in music.

MARY: I wouldn't say that!

EDWARD: There's the most fascinating group she's listening to. What's it called?

MARY: In X.S.

EDWARD: Capital X Capital S. Isn't that delightful? You should really hear them. [*To* MARY.] Give Helen a listen.

MARY: OK.

HELEN: No, please. That's all right.

EDWARD: Do try, Learned. It's a new experience.

HELEN: I don't care for that kind of music, as you know, Edward.

EDWARD: We must all try to embrace new pleasures, my dear. Just because Dr Jarvis wouldn't have allowed it into Parvus House doesn't mean we have to follow suit. Mary here has been instrumental in enlarging my perceptions. [*Extending the headphones.*] Passing on a young people's world of joy and flexibility.

MARY [*to* HELEN]: That's OK. We don't all have to like the same things, do we?

HELEN: Actually Mr Damson does not particularly like this kind of music himself. He described it to me only last week in rather different terms.

EDWARD: Did I? What?

HELEN: Nigsky noise.

MARY: What's that mean?

HELEN: Nigger.

MARY [*embarrassed*]: Oh.

EDWARD [*to her*]: Nig-nogs. Wogs. Yobs . . . The jungle, my dear. Angry apes! . . . The only standard left.

[*He laughs. Both girls leave in confusion.*]

HELEN [*to* PHILIP]: I know now your father is inside you. I've seen his vehemence. I can only pray he kept everything else for himself.

EDWARD [*sitting again, heavily, with his glass of vodka*]: Smish-smesh! History of the world! Yes.

HELEN: Especially, for me, one thing. The most hateful of all his qualities –

PHILIP: What?

HELEN: Secrecy. Compulsive secrecy . . . You've asked me, over and over, when I first knew of your existence. Do you know? – The day your book arrived from Illinois. Your dissertation.

PHILIP [*startled*]: What do you mean – only *then*?

HELEN: Exactly.

PHILIP: *Just last year?!*

HELEN: That's right.

PHILIP: Jesus!

[*Light change.* EDWARD, *still seated, takes* PHILIP's *book of dramatic criticism out of a large buff envelope and examines it.*]

HELEN: He took it out before he realized what it was.

PHILIP: With *his* last name on the jacket.

HELEN: Yes.

PHILIP: Was he angry?

EDWARD [*fiercely*]: The gall! The sheer gall of it! . . . The fucking gall!

HELEN [*to* EDWARD]: What's the matter?

EDWARD: It's *mine*! Mine only! I coined it! I never gave him permission to use it.

HELEN: What on earth are you talking about?

[*He thrusts the book at her, glaring.*]

What is this?

EDWARD: What does it look like? Criticism, of course. What else would it ever be? More academic refuse. [*Mocking.*] *A New Function for Criticism.*

HELEN [*looking at the cover*]: By Philip Damson . . . Is this a pseudonym?

EDWARD: Pseudo, yes.

HELEN: I don't understand.

EDWARD: Isn't it obvious?

73

HELEN: Not to me. Who is this man?

EDWARD: As you see: a professor. One of the endless tribe.

HELEN: Answer me, please.

[*He turns away from her.*]

Edward . . . who is this man?

[*Pause.*]

EDWARD: The word is son.

[*Pause.*]

HELEN: How old?

EDWARD: Old enough to be a critic.

HELEN [*crying out*]: Tell me!

EDWARD [*turning on her*]: What's it matter? It's years ago! . . .
A holiday. A mistake. They happen every hour.

HELEN: You mean that girl you went with to Greece? . . .
Who lived in Cambridge?

EDWARD: Yes. That's who I mean . . . [*Pause.*] It's bad
Victorian fiction, isn't it. *The Concealed Son* . . . Drunken
artist, dedicated wife. [*Less harshly.*] Look, telling you
would have hurt far more. Me not wanting children –
having one all the time.

HELEN [*sarcastic*]: So you were sparing me?

EDWARD: I do my best, Helen. You may not think so. You
prefer always to be the judge: Athena to the end. Good
God, just think of all our time together. All those years!
Isn't it plain how little, how provably *little* the boy –

[*Short pause. He freezes.*]

PHILIP [*finishing the thought*]: 'Meant to me'?

HELEN [*to* PHILIP]: You made me do this, remember. You
insisted!

PHILIP [*tightly*]: Please . . . How can it hurt now?

[*Pause.*]

Even if they'd stayed together they could never have made
a home. Edward Damson and Iris Paley – a little secretary
working for Pembroke College. They *both* wanted to split
– not just him. I used to have fantasies about declaring

myself to him, when he came to America with a play. Perhaps at a Broadway first night. 'Good evening, sir. I am your son. My name is Philip.' . . . Of course, in actuality, it took me years even to write to him — and then only when I had something solid to offer, like a book . . . I wrote my address prominently on the inside.

HELEN [*gently*]: How you must have longed for his reply.

PHILIP [*shyly*]: Tell me, did he in fact ever read it? . . . Be honest.

> [*Contemptuously* EDWARD *tosses the book into the basket of other books.*]

EDWARD: Generation, my dear, is a form of amoebic dysentery. Man's lot, if he reproduces at all, is to give birth to his own parasites. You may consider yourself lucky you've been kept from risk.

PHILIP: My God!

HELEN: Entirely typical of his later style of address. All the same, when he suddenly went off to America, I hoped perhaps he might have changed his mind and seen you.

PHILIP [*surprised*]: When was this?

HELEN: A month after your book arrived.

> [EDWARD *rises.*]

PHILIP: He went to America after the *I.R.E.* fiasco? I thought he stayed here in total retirement.

HELEN: It was the only time he left. One trip.

PHILIP [*urgently*]: But why? What reason did he give for going?

EDWARD: A lecture tour of the East Coast. Five weeks fully paid — by the most out-of-touch foundation in America. They don't seem to have heard I've become a leper.

HELEN: Will you go?

EDWARD: Should I?

HELEN: Why not? You always enjoy America, don't you?

EDWARD: Do I?

HELEN: I don't really know: you've never taken me there.

EDWARD: Wisely. It's not for the learned. Less so with every passing day.

[*He goes to a rack in the corner and takes a coat.*]

HELEN: Well, perhaps while you're there you'll be able to see . . .

EDWARD: What? See who?

HELEN: Your son. You have his address now.

[EDWARD *leaves without replying.*]

PHILIP: I never heard anything about this.

HELEN [*to* PHILIP, *looking after* EDWARD]: No.

PHILIP: What happened?

HELEN: He went.

[EDWARD *re-enters, taking off his coat.*]

And came back within a week.

PHILIP: All that way just for a week?

HELEN: Yes.

PHILIP: What happened?

EDWARD: It did not please.

HELEN [*to* EDWARD]: But the tour. You just gave that up?

EDWARD: As you see.

HELEN: I don't understand. Did they cancel it? . . .

[EDWARD *takes out a bottle of vodka and pours himself a glass.*]

[*Sharper.*] Edward, please! Why are you back so soon?

[*He walks out of the room on to the terrace with his drink.*]

PHILIP: He never answered?

HELEN: Oh, yes. A few days later all was revealed.

[JO–BETH *comes on to the terrace: a young American girl wearing a T-shirt and jeans torn at the knee. Her blonde hair is tied in a head-band.*]

PHILIP: How?

HELEN: Through a girl. The last of his Back-Packlettes. A kind of late-flowering hippie. One of those endless girls you see wandering around Greece, their clothes torn deliberately. This one was called Jo–Beth.

EDWARD [*kissing her sloppily*]: A beautiful name. Profoundly Early-American!

HELEN: She'd brought him up from the harbour one morning. He'd apparently been drinking with her in a bar most of the night. He'd been too frail to climb the steps. She'd managed to get him on a donkey.

[*He comes back into the living-room on the girl's arm, hair tousled, the worse for wear.*]

JO-BETH [*to* HELEN]: Quite a job it was too!

HELEN: Yes, well I'm most grateful. I'm Helen Damson.

JO-BETH: Hi.

EDWARD: This is Jo-Beth. It doesn't actually suit her.

JO-BETH: I guess we need some coffee – if you wouldn't mind.

HELEN: I'll get it. [*Moving to one side: to* PHILIP.] And from the kitchen I heard everything.

JO-BETH: I thought you liked my name.

EDWARD: It's too puritanical for you. Suggests carrot cake and gingham bonnets. I shall rechristen you 'Wowie'.

JO-BETH: 'Wowie'?

EDWARD: The archetypal wow-girl! It's your most frequent expression.

JO-BETH: Thanks a lot.

EDWARD: No, it's good. Noun and verb simultaneously – typical American solution: 'you're a wow!' and 'you wow me!' . . . It's almost as versatile as the great American monosyllable. D'you know what that is?

JO-BETH: What?

EDWARD: 'Shit'.

JO-BETH: Very funny.

EDWARD: I'm serious. It's the most frequently used word in the American vocabulary, especially by the educated: 'I've done the shopping and all that shit', – 'I've had all the shit I can take', 'It's really shitty weather', 'Shit, man!', 'Holy shit!' It's great. This saves them hours they used to waste in precision.

[JO-BETH *laughs*.]

JO-BETH: You're just mad because of your son.

EDWARD [*startled*]: What? . . . What do you say?

JO-BETH: Your son – what you told me last night.

EDWARD: What are you talking about?

JO-BETH: You know. Like seeing him there.

[HELEN *becomes attentive*, PHILIP *also*.]

You told me the whole story last night! About *seeing* him in America.

PHILIP: *What?*

JO-BETH: Don't say you were too smashed to remember.

EDWARD [*warningly*]: I don't know what you're talking about, Wowie.

JO-BETH: Well, Jesus, I'm not making it up! Do you deny you spoke to me last night about seeing your son in America?

EDWARD: I think it's you who must have been smashed.

JO-BETH: You said you went out to Illinois especially to find your son, and –

EDWARD [*sharp*]: *Be quiet!*

PHILIP: Oh, God! What?

[JO-BETH *shuts up, suddenly alarmed.* KATINA *comes in with a tray of steaming coffee and cups, which she gives to* HELEN *then leaves.* HELEN *joins* EDWARD *and* JO-BETH, *carrying the tray.*]

EDWARD [*to* HELEN]: She's not staying.

HELEN: I'm sorry?

EDWARD: She has remembered an appointment. She has to leave us.

JO-BETH: I do?

EDWARD: Didn't you just say you had remembered an appointment?

[*Pause.*]

JO-BETH [*to* HELEN]: I guess I haven't got time for coffee this morning. I'm sorry I bothered you.

HELEN: That's all right.

EDWARD: You know your way back to the harbour?

JO-BETH [cold]: I can find it . . . [To HELEN.] It's been nice meeting you.

HELEN: Thank you for bringing him back.

JO-BETH: Thank the donkey. I didn't do anything. [To EDWARD.] So long.

> [EDWARD does not reply. JO-BETH shrugs and goes. Pause.]

HELEN: You want coffee?

EDWARD: No.

> [He pours himself a large vodka.]

HELEN: You saw him.

PHILIP: He didn't. He couldn't have.

HELEN: Didn't you?

PHILIP: It was just a fantasy!

EDWARD: After a fashion.

HELEN: Meaning?

> [EDWARD drinks off his glass.]
>
> Meaning, Edward? . . .

EDWARD: I observed him. Checked him out, as they say. Look, New York was unbearable. A Caribbean Congo. I had to get out . . . My lectures weren't starting for another few days. Illinois was only two hours away by plane. I thought suddenly, why not?

HELEN: Visit him?

EDWARD: I'd no notion of what I wanted. I just went.

HELEN: To his college?

EDWARD: Flavourless, faceless town. I found myself an hotel. Registered under some fake name. In the lobby I found leaflets with my real one. They announced a seminar to be held that night. On the works of Edward Damson. Conducted by guess who.

PHILIP: Oh, Christ!

EDWARD: No less than one Philip Damson. I made a plan.

Sit at the back. If he pleased, make myself known at the end. If he didn't, just steal away. No one would ever know I was there.

[*Pause. He sits.*]

PHILIP [*frantic*]: Yes? And? . . . *What?*

EDWARD: Eight o'clock I went to the lecture hall. Some fake Gothic structure on the campus. About a third full. Then the professors entered. Two dried-up sticks and my son. Twenty-eight years old – about to become a stick himself.

PHILIP: Jesus!

EDWARD: It was the first time I'd ever seen him. I was reminded at once of his mother – that prim face of hers, which had attracted me for about a week. He had that antiseptic neatness of American academics: bow-tie, button-down collar, short sight from reading too many polysyllabic adjectives.

[PHILIP *looks away sharply.*]

HELEN: I warned you.

PHILIP [*tight*]: Go on.

EDWARD: The two professors read endless papers about me: 'Damson and the Crisis in Post-Modern Dramaturgy', 'Damson and Presentational Identity'. The whole place virtually had lockjaw from yawning. Then my son rose to speak. At least he was comprehensible. He appeared to feel some obligation to interest his audience: blood will out, I suppose. He was still unbearable.

HELEN: What do you mean?

EDWARD: Because of what he was doing . . . Apologizing.

HELEN: For what?

EDWARD: Me. For me. For playwrights everywhere. 'Hey folks, listen! Live theatre can be fun: honest! My old dad isn't that boring once ya get used to him!' . . . Excusing me to children, who only know television or movies, and *want* only them! . . . 'Movies', the ultimate kiddie word! Things that move continuously, dragging their eye-balls without

their will, permitting them no selection, no reflection! The
car-chase, the man-chase, the car-crash, the man-crash, the
exploding gun, the exploding house – the surface of violence that brings no release . . . My son offered *Me* as an
alternative. [*Speaking as if to children.*] 'Do you know what
a playwright does? He makes you see with your *ears*! He
turns sounds into sight! Now that's *real* magic, isn't it?' . . .
They simply sat there and yawned. He declaimed my
speeches – as badly as only an academic could – and they
yawned again. Their infant ears could not receive speeches
longer than a minute. Their infant eyes, like those of
animals, could not see what was not before them. Finally
row by row the audience got up and left.

PHILIP [*distressed*]: It's true. There was that seminar . . . I'm
not much of an actor . . .

EDWARD: Row after row of gum-chewing boys and girls,
slouching off into the night! And watching them, I suddenly had this blinding revelation. I saw exactly who I was.
Merely the quaint priest of a spent religion, shuffling
around the altar, trying to stoke a sacred fire that had gone
out unnoticed. The Drama is dead.

PHILIP: No! . . . Did he *say* that?

EDWARD: I'm telling you the truth according to America,
by which we all live now. The world doesn't need theatre
any more. It has been dismissed by the audience I thought
of as eternal. Nothing is eternal: not even the imagination.
They all sit now goggling before screens, raped and starv-
ing, and not even knowing it. Everywhere the dragon-
wing of the literal has o'er-spread the earth. [*Pause.*] All
this, unwittingly, my earnest little son had shown me.

   [*Pause. He rises.*]
I went outside into the dark, and watched him through the
window – standing there in an almost empty hall, sur-
rounded by pasty experts, all huddled together in a faith
that had once been universal and then simply shrank until

it died of disuse. [*Bitterly.*] *My religion!* – which I thought was imperishable! – now just a subject for dissection, conducted by eunuchs who couldn't earn a living any other way.

[PHILIP *groans.*]

I watched his mouth, endlessly opening and shutting, giving artificial respiration to the obviously extinct. He was like some Icon of Irrelevance! And I, on the other side of the glass, *irrelevant too!* Our images fused into one – the Dramatist and the Professor of Drama: both unneeded. Just Nobodies in Nowhere U.S.A – which is now Everywhere.

[*Pause. He moves closer to* PHILIP, *and speaks intimately.*]

I shouted through the window at him. Of course he couldn't hear me. 'Stop your yap, for God's sake. The soldier's pole is fallen! . . . I at least created theatre and wasted my life. What are *you* – who merely spend it commenting on a waster?'

[*Pause.*]

Then I left for home. If that is what one can call this.

[*He turns, grabs the vodka and stumbles out on to the terrace.*]

HELEN: I sat there with a new feeling. A sudden overwhelming urge to rebuke this man as hard as I could. Wasted his life. That's what he said. Wasted his life . . . All the other insults I could bear – but not this. [*Pause.*] That's when I did it. That same day.

PHILIP: What? Helen, what did you do?

HELEN: I remembered the excitement I felt when I found that first Perseus scene he left on my pillow. When he turned me into Athena. I remembered the pain when I received the second one, dismissing me. I knew the only words that could reach him now had to be *written*.

PHILIP: You mean – you wrote him a letter?

HELEN: No.

PHILIP: What then? . . .

HELEN: His way.

PHILIP: A scene? You wrote him a *scene*?

[*She goes calmly to the desk and takes out a final large envelope.*]

HELEN: I took a piece of his special paper, went upstairs to my room, locked the door and sat down to write. I kept thinking, Now I'm alone with him, as I can never be in the flesh. And suddenly it began to flow — with such force I couldn't believe it. Like blood leaving a wound. As if, for one afternoon, I was empowered.

[*Light change.* EDWARD *swigs from the bottle. Dusk falls.*]

As evening came, I went downstairs — and left it for him. On his altar.

[*She places the envelope prominently on the desk.*]

Then I watched — hidden in the doorway.

[*A grim music begins, low.* PHILIP *moves towards the desk, as the light grows more menacing. At the same time* EDWARD *comes in from the terrace, holding his bottle of vodka. He sees the envelope, picks it up, extracts and unfolds the scene, written in her hand in blue. He holds it out in front of him so that* PHILIP *standing beside him, can see it too.*]

EDWARD: What's this? . . . [*Reading.*] One day — one day too many — Athena *finally* wearied of Perseus.

PHILIP [*reading*]: The sound from his drunken mouth, continually assaulting her. [*To* HELEN.] My God!

EDWARD: What *is* this? . . . [*He reads on.*]

[*Music grows, drunken in sound at the start. The cliffs part again, and the ramp lowers.* PERSEUS *enters, walking in a disordered way. As usual their voices are on tape.*]

PHILIP [*reading*]: Enter Perseus. He is blear-eyed. No longer strutting, but staggering — not one vestige of a Hero left.

[ATHENA *follows him, carrying spear and shield.*]

ATHENA [*angrily*]: I see you, Perseus!

[PERSEUS *wobbles to a stop, staring straight out front.*]

ATHENA: Perseus Unaided! . . . Do you remember what you were when I found you? — Desperate! Lusting for triumph, though never able to claim it on your own!

EDWARD [*raging*]: Now look! Now look – What *is* this?

ATHENA: You prayed to me! 'Help! Help me, Hellenica!' Remember? I came willingly. I pulled you out of terror. Set you free to fly up to your glory! . . . What did I ask in return? *One gift!* The gift of the Gorgon's head – source of paralysis – to set in my shield and keep from harming you, for ever! *Where is it?* [*Raising it.*] Look: empty! . . . You kept it! Do you not know the fate of him who keeps that head for himself? The man who keeps the Gorgon – *becomes* the Gorgon!

[*Hissing louder.*]

PHILIP: Oh, yes! . . . Yes! . . . Oh, Helen!

ATHENA [*to* EDWARD]: Come here. This is the Shield of Showing. The total image of your life! Approach now and see it! See it! – see it! – see it! – *Edward!*

HELEN [*together with* ATHENA] *Edward!*

[PERSEUS *falls to his knees as* EDWARD *moves mesmerized, holding the paper, towards the shield.* HELEN *takes over the speaking from* ATHENA.]

HELEN: Look first at the land around you, you have laid to waste. Your *own* Island of Immobility.

[ATHENA *tilts the shield and* EDWARD *stares directly into it.* HELEN *continues to speak with accumulating and fierce distress.*]

See the figures you might have warmed to life – standing now rigid, grey and dying . . . Look, Edward. [ATHENA *tilts the shield towards* PHILIP.] Do you see him there, your son? Philip. Rejected at birth. Rejected again. Twice, twice rejected! A boy whose only crime was adoration: the greatest gift a father can receive! . . . He ran thousands of miles from you, to save you anger. Stayed there, in for him a wilderness, singing your praises! But you had to hunt him: all that distance, just to stand in the dark and fix these eyes on him, and curse him. Do you think that can ever be forgiven? Keep looking. Keep looking hard. Your wife stands there too.

[ATHENA *turns the shield above to mirror* HELEN. EDWARD *moves, staring up at it to see her reflection.*]

She could have shone. She could have been a scholar. One drop of the encouragement she offered you would have grown her. But you didn't want that . . . [*Pause.*] It was her own fault, yes. She surrendered all her ambitions for herself – offered them freely. But you *took* them, my friend – *too willingly! As your right!* Took them as you took her fertility. 'Not for you,' you said, 'real children. You'll have others – paper children.' But what did she get in the end? Something so foul, she couldn't look! . . . She sat beside you, that night in the theatre, so shamed. So barren. Made barren. Turned barren by you. *A womb of stone!* [*Pause.*] And then today she heard your voice. 'I've wasted my life,' it said. So then, did *she*? . . . [*Hard.*] Yes. Yes, she did. I did. I have. [*Silence.*] The art cannot die, Edward. Ever. Just the artist. Just the lover. Just the husband. Just the father. [*With contemptuous fury.*] Perseus Unaided – you will never fly again.

[ATHENA *withdraws into darkness: the cliffs and the screens close after her. Below, downstage,* PERSEUS, *broken, crawls off painfully, lying on his side. The music fades. The light becomes naturalistic. Night has fallen. Husband and wife stare at each other: he still holds the paper.*]

HELEN: I'm leaving you, Edward. This is the last time we'll speak. Now you can live completely as you've chosen. Drink with your girls, and denounce the world. And when they have left, you can have your snakes for company. Listen to *them*.

EDWARD: Do you mean this?

HELEN: Tomorrow. First boat.

[*He turns sharply away from her.*]

[*To* PHILIP.] I hadn't meant to say it. Not out loud to his face. But suddenly I knew I wanted it. To get away from him as far as possible. Never, never to hear him again. [*To*

EDWARD, *savagely.*] *I can't wait!* [*To* PHILIP.] He said nothing. Just walked out on to the terrace. And shut himself away in the dark.

[EDWARD *does what she describes, still holding her written scene, and gently closes the shutters upon himself. Pause.*]

Then everything stopped. He stayed there. And I in here. Both in silence – the shutters between us. I sat so stiff I thought a bone must snap. A moon came up. An hour passed – two – God knows how many. Until at last, when I thought the world would never move again –

[*The shutters open slowly, to reveal* EDWARD *again.*]

He came to me.

[*He enters the room and moves to his wife.*]

[*In distress.*] I wish I could have realized clearly how bad he was. How deeply I'd cut him . . . I saw only what I wanted. His need. That need for me he'd had when we first ran away together.

[EDWARD *falls ceremoniously on his knees before her.*]

[*Desperately.*] I thought I saw it. I thought I'd found it again – there in his eyes – when he knelt . . . *I thought that's what it was!*

[*He takes her hand and places it on his head.*]

EDWARD [*softly*]: Us . . . Us . . . I beg you. Your mad husband begs.

HELEN: What?

EDWARD: Restore us.

HELEN: I don't understand.

EDWARD: Bring back our days together.

HELEN: There's no back. You know that.

EDWARD: At least try. Only you can.

HELEN: I?

EDWARD: Give me *something*. A symbol to start.

HELEN: I don't know what you mean . . .

EDWARD: Cleanse me. Physically. Wash me. Do you remember when you did? When I danced – you cleaned me first . . . Do it now. It can be a start.

HELEN: It's too late.

EDWARD: Try, Learned. Try.

HELEN: Go away! . . . Please!

EDWARD: Make a ritual. Brave and learned lady: create one. Wash your husband. Wipe away his wrongs to you. Forgive him on his body! . . . Help me atone.

HELEN [to PHILIP]: On and on. You had to hear it.

EDWARD: Try.

HELEN: Me shaking.

EDWARD: For us both.

HELEN: Him kneeling. Saying 'restore'.

EDWARD: Make it right.

HELEN: 'Bring it back . . . Help me atone.' [In anguish.] He knew how much I wanted to.

EDWARD: Please . . .

HELEN: His face near me. After so long. Saying 'please'. Just 'please' – after so long.

[Pause. She stares down at him.]

How was I to know?

[EDWARD watches her pleadingly.]

EDWARD: Wash my body. In your patience. In your love.

[Pause. She hardly knows what to say.]

Yes?

[She nods.]

No lights. Turn on the shower. I'll come to you.

HELEN [to PHILIP]: And I went.

PHILIP: To the shower?

HELEN: A little one, along the passage there. I went in the dark; the moonlight shining through the glass roof. I turned the handle, and then waited.

[We hear the sound of water splashing. EDWARD divests himself of his shirt, then goes to the desk – takes the razor blade out of the mat-knife – and, holding it between his fingers, leaves the room.]

He came to me naked. He stepped into the shower and

handed me the soap, like the last time. Greek olive-oil soap, into which he – he'd . . .

PHILIP: Put a blade. From the mat-knife . . . Yes?

HELEN: And I soaped him . . . 'Harder,' he said. 'All over. Don't be niminy-wiminy!' . . . And I did it – harder and harder – happy suddenly, laughing as the water wet me too, my dress and hair . . . Till I felt in the water, which was tepid, something hotter . . .

[*She stares at her fingers, starting to shake.*]

I ran back in here. Saw on my dress the stains . . .

[*The shower stops. A silence.*]

And then he followed.

[*Slowly* EDWARD *enters, naked save for a huge white towel. He stands before his wife, shuddering. Presently a crimson stain appears on the towel from underneath it: slowly it spreads across his chest and stomach. Suddenly he seizes off the desk the scene which she wrote as* ATHENA – *and thrusts it at her urgently.*]

HELEN: My scene. The one I'd written. On the back of it now – his answer . . . That's what he'd been doing behind the shutters. *Writing to me*, in the moonlight!

[*She hands the paper to* PHILIP. *We see her handwriting in the blue ink and, on the back,* EDWARD's – *in red. Her husband stares at her wildly as his son reads it aloud. Some of his blood runs on the white floor.*]

PHILIP [*reading*]: Justice. Justice clear and clean. See it, Learned: a terrible thing to look on. And a right one. Justice for us both.

[HELEN *looks at* EDWARD *in horror.* PHILIP *continues, badly shaken.*]

I have taken for you the revenge you need. This is my gift to you: the Sacred Gift of Vengeance. I have made you the instrument of my atonement. Be appeased. This is the blood that cures. [*Tenderly.*] Dear girl, my sins are many and vile. I beg you, my injured lady, maimed and learned love, accept this maiming in return. So I give up the Gorgon.

[HELEN *stands rooted to the ground, her hands before her face.* EDWARD *approaches her.*]

EDWARD [*hoarsely and urgently*]: Accept it . . . Accept it . . . [*He touches her hands.*] Accept.

[*Violently,* HELEN *pushes him away. He staggers back and falls on to the floor. Then, suddenly, he smiles in a terrible grimace, turns over, and crawls slowly in agony through the arch of the desk on to the dark terrace where shakily he stands.*]

HELEN [*watching this: to* PHILIP]: I couldn't stir. Just stood and watched him crawl over the grass, trailing that robe of blood towards the cliff. I heard my own voice screaming out of me I don't know what. Words of hate – 'Damn you! Damn you to hell!' – all kinds of hate . . . He heard me. At the very edge he stopped and squatted there. Then, trembling with pain, reached up slowly with both arms into the moonlight. Straining at the sky and waving, like a man trying to fly. [*Pause.*] And then – as if it were a sudden choice – he just bowed himself over the rim. Simply bowed and fell. Far down on to the lava, sharper than any razor.

[EDWARD *bows down. The shutters gently close. Pause.*]

Then I could move. I ran to the village, banged on the doors. Men ran back with me, scrambled down and carried him up – naked and stinking of drink. [*Pause.*] There was never a thought it wasn't an accident. They looked at me with pity.

[*A siren is heard in the distance: the light changes back to the present moment.* KATINA *enters.* PHILIP *stands stunned.*]

KATINA: *To karavi erhete. Ine piso ston faro.* (The boat is coming. It's round the headland.)

HELEN [*to* PHILIP]: Your boat is coming round the headland.

KATINA: *O kyrios ehi mono misi ora.* (The gentleman has half an hour.)

HELEN: You have little time to get down to the harbour. [*To* KATINA.] *Efgaristo.*

    [KATINA *goes. Pause.*]

    [*To* PHILIP.] But you're not going, of course.

PHILIP [*numb*]: What? . . .

HELEN: You're staying here. You can wire the college, resigning. Say you're ill.

PHILIP [*bewildered*]: Excuse me? . . .

HELEN: You have to write the book now. That's your priority.

PHILIP: But you can't . . . You can't publish this!

HELEN: Why not?

PHILIP: It's impossible!

HELEN: Why?

PHILIP: It'll *finish* him! . . . There won't *be* a playwright any more. Just a freak. That's all there'll be left! That's all they'll talk about. That's all they'll remember, for ever . . . The man will be destroyed! Trivialized! . . . *Erased!* – He'll be *erased*!

HELEN [*cold*]: Exactly.

    [*Pause.*]

PHILIP: What do you mean?

HELEN: That'll be our gift to him. Yours and mine together. *Our* Sacred Gift. [*Pause.*] This has to be avenged, Philip. It can't be left unanswered.

PHILIP: Avenged? . . . '*Avenged?*' . . . I don't believe it! . . .

    [*Pause.*]

HELEN: Do you know what it's like to lie at night, week after week, months, not sleeping? Feeling that blood between your fingers? That's what he wanted. Just that. What he designed for me.

PHILIP: No!

    [*She speaks now with a terrible calm.*]

HELEN: Oh, yes! Remember what he said? 'There are such things as unforgivable acts – beyond the pale of pardon.' I said, 'No, I'll never believe that.' What did he say *then*? 'I'll make you . . . I'll *make* you.' [*Pause.*] Well, he has. *That's what he's done.* I believe it now. *Oh, God, I do!* [*In huge distress.*] The obscenity! The *obscenity*. Out of atonement to make *that*! . . . All I want now is to hurt him. Hurt and hurt and hurt, for ever and ever. [*Pause.*] God knows. I did my best to keep you away. Nothing would work, you would come! [*Mimicking him.*] 'Give me my father! I want my father!' [*Cold.*] Well, now you have him. You can show him to the world.

PHILIP: No.

HELEN: You have to. You swore.

PHILIP: No.

HELEN [*desperately*]: You swore! On that desk. You swore!

[*Suddenly he cries out with a fierceness he has never shown before.*]

PHILIP: *No! – No! – No! – No!* . . . No one will write this story! Ever! [*Urgently.*] There's another life for you, Helen. Go back to England and live it. It's your only hope.

[*The wind is heard faintly.*]

HELEN: Give me that page, please.

[*She holds out her hand for the paper which* PHILIP *still holds.*]

It will serve for the cover. My scene reproduced on the front, his reply on the back . . . One of the professors will write it, no doubt. They're not famous for refusing fortunes.

[*Pause.*]

PHILIP: This book will be your dance. Your Dance of Rightful Stamping.

HELEN [*implacably*]: Please.

[*He thrusts the page into her hand.*]

PHILIP: Well, not mine. I'm going back to America, to my

dull college. And I'm going to make the best lectures I know how to – on *him*. And he'll *glint* for those students, I promise you.

[*He looks suddenly at the empty terrace.*]

[*With deep emotion.*] You'll glint – as you did for me, Edward! I'm going to make you live! . . . And you can stand outside that same window again, you bastard – and watch.

[*The siren sounds, very loud.* KATINA *calls from offstage.*]

KATINA: *To pilo araxe! Prepi na fighi amesos!* (The boat has docked. He must go at once.)

[*He turns to* HELEN.]

PHILIP: The truth is, you must forgive him or die.

[*He picks up his suitcase and walks away into the dark, back to the corner where he was discovered at the beginning.* HELEN *goes to the basket of books, takes some up and examines them.*

The wind now begins to rise a little. A low chord is heard, prolonging itself, and the light changes significantly to an ominous twilight.

The cliffs and shutters part, the ramp lowers, and EDWARD, *in his old sweater and trousers, but now wearing a death-mask of his own face, slowly walks down it and on to the desk.*

In elaborate, weaving slow motion he begins to stamp the steps of Clytemnestra's triumph. HELEN *does not look at him but stands rigid, downstage, staring straight ahead. The theatre is filled with the sound of her dead husband whispering wooingly on tape.*]

EDWARD's voice: Dance! . . . Dance! . . . Dance! . . . Dance! . . . Dance! . . .

[*The light comes up on* PHILIP. HELEN *produces a letter from him and holds it out, reading it.*]

PHILIP: You are your father's daughter. Honour him now, better than he honoured himself. He could never forgive – with far less cause.

EDWARD's voice [*whispering*]: Do it now. I'm waiting . . . Make that book, and dance!

PHILIP: We must be bigger than our ancestors, or we have no point. Remember?

EDWARD's voice: I'm watching . . . Do it, Learned. *Now!*

[HELEN *stands indecisively, holding books in one hand, the letter in the other. Slowly* EDWARD *dances on the desk in the half-light.*]

PHILIP: Won't you reply? *Please!* Answer me!

EDWARD's voice [*more and more insistently*]: Come on now, girl! Will you avoid all your life? *Stamp!* . . . On my mouth! On my fame! . . . Kill me for ever in your world!

PHILIP [*urgently*]: Helen, where are you?

EDWARD's voice: Clean that blood the only way there is! Destroy me and *dance!*

PHILIP: *Helen? . . . Helen, please reply!*

EDWARD's voice: Do it, Learned, do it. For God's sake, *make that book!*

HELEN [*abruptly calling out*]: *Katina!*

[*She throws the books and Philip's letter back into the basket.* KATINA *enters.*]

[*Briskly pointing to the basket.*] *Pare afta ta vivlia. Katastrepseta.* (Take these books away. Destroy them.)

[*Insistently she makes the gesture of throwing them away. The housekeeper looks at her in astonishment – then drags the basket offstage by its handle. And now decisively* HELEN *produces the paper with her scene written on one side and* EDWARD's *response on the other. Firmly she raises it above her head and shows it to her husband's spirit.*]

HELEN [*calling out to it*]: *Here!* Look now! Look now, Edward Damson!

[*She tears it across, scattering the pieces on the floor. The*

music ceases. EDWARD *stops dancing and freezes.* PHILIP
*holds out a letter from her and she speaks stiffly, as he reads
it.*] There will be no book. No one but you and I will
ever know.

PHILIP: Thank God!

[*The ramp withdraws into the cliff of lava. The shutters slide
together. There now ensues a long, long silence.* HELEN
*stands downstage, her eyes closed in relief. Behind her on his
desk* EDWARD *stands, completely still. The silence hangs
over the stage until it is barely endurable – and then suddenly
the masked figure stamps a foot. It is heard quite softly at first
– then another comes, louder – and* EDWARD, *rocking from
side to side, starts all over again his terrible stamping dance.
The noise of it grows in the theatre.*]

HELEN [*appalled*]: Is it to go on for ever? . . . *Does* it go on
for ever? . . . Always? . . . Everywhere? . . .

[*She raises her voice.*]

I forgive you! . . . I forgive you! . . . I will! . . . I will! . . .

[*She turns and moves upstage towards her husband. The light
concentrates on them.*]

HELEN: I forgive you! I forgive you! . . . I do! I do! . . .

[*And now she begins to move faster and faster around the desk
as* EDWARD's *stamping becomes ever louder and more
savage.*]

HELEN [*desperately, urgently, trying to obliterate the sound as she
runs*]: I forgive! . . . I forgive! . . . I forgive! . . . I forgive!
. . . I forgive! . . . I forgive! . . . I forgive! . . . I forgive! . . .
I forgive! . . . I forgive! . . . I FORGIVE!

[*The light goes out. All sound ceases.*]

END OF PLAY